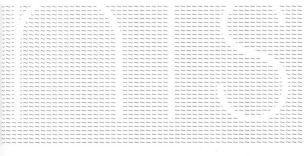

CONTEMPORARY TEXTILES

the fabric of fine art

**black dog
publishing**
london uk

everything is the stuff of art

jann haworth

"Everything is the stuff of art". Tony Caro nailed us with this declaration as we were watching Phillip King working in the sculpture studio at St Martin's School of Art. We were working up a collaboration between ourselves—Slade painting students— and the Sculpture Department of St Martins. It was late 1962, early 1963. Yoko was due in for a gig with her partner, students were collecting bicycles for her, which she wouldn't use; and the *Black Bag* piece that she did with her husband was rumoured to be on the menu.

"The stuff of art"… he didn't just mean everything was ours for subject: from abstract ideas, random mark-making, urinals, beer cans, traditional figuration or mass media popular culture. He was pushing the freedom of materials and process at us. It was a validation that meant a great deal to me.

As an American student at the Slade, I felt increasingly isolated because of gender issues, cultural background and gaps in communication. I had begun to make sculpture in fabric. I had made *Flowers*, a bouquet of body parts on stems coming out of a ceramic sewage pipe; *Dog* made of an old black coat I got from Portobello Road with wooden Georgian furniture legs; and *Wardrobe* with wooden clothes and hats made of plates, bowls and random vessels. The best of the reactions to my work had been a mild-mannered indulgence—as one would give to an amusing child—the worst: Eduardo Paolozzi, then a tutor at the Slade, glancing at the work on a rare visit to the painting studio, "cast it in bronze", he'd said. Fortunately, I had the presence of mind to bark after him "I've cast it in cloth!".

I failed to see the barriers between correct materials and incorrect ones—between 'high art' and 'the crafts'. I would hazard a guess that this is a sentiment common to many in this book. We are perplexed that something so obvious and simple as a wild, free use of materials and form can evoke such critical analysis. There are no rules in art. It's as simple as that. As our curators, professors, critics and art historians verbalise, the artist slips sleekly through the fence and is off on another unkempt escapade.

This book is a testimony to the intellectual freedoms of the twentieth century, created in part by the democratisation of information through education, the impact of photography (film, current event documentation, access to the history of art, foreign culture), travel and flight, the conceptual maps of relativity and psychology and the first steps toward the equality of women and ethnic 'minorities'.

We have vaulted away from an art tied to the illustration of gods, myth, narrative and the record of royalty and patrons. We live with the abstract, the emotional, diversified mark-making and impossible to tame materials. We embraced experiment and our mistakes. The nature of the truly creative is rebellion—against what has been, against habit, the norm, our stamina and the limitation of the 'known'. Art is a quest… It is a path into the unknown. You are about to embark.

note from the editor
nadine monem

From their beginnings in craft-art and the decorative, textiles have fast become the fabric of fine art. This book offers a comprehensive introduction to textile art, complete with a rigorous theoretical foundation in the debates surrounding the medium's use, and profiles of the most cutting edge textile work emerging from the contemporary art world today.

Bradley Quinn situates textile art within the wider context of contemporary practice, citing the influences and initiatives that gradually drew the medium into the folds of 'high art'. Going on to discuss a wide selection of artists and their work, "Textiles at the Cutting Edge", offers an insight into the motivations and methods behind some of the best textile art emerging today, told with all the vibrance of Quinn's characteristically lively style. Janis Jefferies takes up some of the themes introduced by Quinn and goes on to offer a robust critical analysis of textiles' history in the ornamental and the decorative. Unpacking various theoretical, political and social motivations behind textiles' increasing prominence in the fine art context, "Contemporary Textiles: the Art Fabric" offers the insight and expertise necessary to fully understand and appreciate the work profiled in this book. And this is where the visual riot begins.

Within each of the four sections of artist profiles there is a staggering range of signifiers, concepts, materials and methods merging and colliding in work from some of the most important fine artists practicing today. The "Drawings" section focuses on the field of embroidery, with Andrea Dezsö's darkly humourous take on the sampler, Jessica Rankin's haunting psycho-cartographic assemblages and Tilleke Schwarz' urban bricolage, offering a first look at some of the most innovative artwork being done with thread and needle. The "Paintings" section profiles artists who work primarily in weaving or otherwise approach textiles with a painterly creative method. Silja Puranen's fantastical and unsettling appliqués on found materials are presented alongside Devorah Sperber's stunning reimaginings of the Old Masters and Tracey Emin's shocking reimaginings of her personal experiences. The legendary Jann Haworth firmly grounds the "Sculptures" section in the tradition of fine art, which goes on to profile some of the most interesting new artists working in soft sculpture and costume. With Janet Echelman's monumental transformations of urban airspace and Matthew Barney's continually surprising transmutations of himself, this section acknowledges a wide range of practices that engage textile fine art in three-dimensions. Finally, "Spaces" presents some of the most exciting installation work to be expressed through a textile medium, with Christo and Jean-Claude's epic environmental work and Yinka Shonibare's startling socio-historical theatre evidencing the startling depth of the textile art installation currently exploding into the gallery space.

The artists in this volume are pushing the boundaries of traditional categories of fine art practice, and in the process they are producing some of the most important, inspiring and evocative work being done today, forever cementing textiles' place at the heart of contemporary art.

bradley quinn

soothing
spaces

Torn fabric, shredded selvedges and tightly-stitched embroidery threads are hallmarks of the textile trade, but in the hands of contemporary artists, they are also raw materials for some of the edgiest artworks produced today. As artists reclaim fibres as contemporary art-forms, they are finding fresh expressions as soft sculptures, woven installations and embroidered paintings. Cutting-edge artworks and tactile fabrics may have once seemed irreconcilably diverse, but today, there are threads that bind.

For many years, attempts to elevate fibre-based forms to the lofty heights of fine art were routinely overturned. The art world is a stock exchange of status and chic, and textiles were traditionally dismissed as functional forms or decorative expressions. Yet, throughout history, the exchanges between them have been undeniable, because neither exists independently of the other. Themes from nature, society and spirituality are expressed in both mediums, and movements such as Realism, Surrealism, Avant-Gardism and Abstraction are common to each. Their congruencies are not just surface deep; scrape away the layers of paint and primer, and the fabric underpinning them comes clearly into view.

As Modern Art aligned with movements such as Fluxus, feminist art, Process Art and performance art, fibre-based works featured on contemporary agendas for the first time. American artist Robert Morris broke new ground in 1958, when he layered felt fabrics, slit them horizontally and mounted them on a gallery wall, then cited cutting and draping as artistic processes. In Japan, avant-garde artist Atsuko Tanaka wore a textile embedded with multi-coloured flashing lights onstage, and created an enormous red satin dress with sleeves that extended more than nine metres wide. Beat Generation artist Bruce Connor featured textile objects in his pop-culture 'protest' art, while artists such as Barbara Kruger, Mimi Smith and Judy Chicago transformed tactile materials into vanguards of the feminist genre. Ann Hamilton's works combine textile forms with sculptures, installations and performances; a process shared by Louise Bourgeois, who expressed her lifetime affinity with textiles relatively late in her career. Christo's unique oeuvre treats textiles as mega-materials, revealing that they can reshape whole landscapes as well as define architectural space.

At the dawn of the twenty-first century, textiles gained currency among a new generation. Artists such as Lucy Orta, Andrea Zittel, Jorge Pardo, Tracey Emin, Rosemarie Trockel, Do-Ho Suh and Yinka Shonibare fused textiles with a diverse range of media, creating unexpected forms as a result. Their artworks, like those of their contemporaries, reveal how textiles bridge diverse narratives more easily than most other media, and spark interpretations that are both literal and metaphorical.

The relationship between textiles and contemporary art is forging fresh directions today, and it demands a new dialogue. Divided into five sections, the text that follows charts this exciting interface by bridging traditional techniques and contemporary expressions. As textiles find a fresh voice within contemporary art, their presence reveals that the cutting edge of art is not necessarily the shock of the new, but the soft, sensuous forms inspired by fabrics from traditional times. Whether stitched across supple surfaces or cut deeply into dense fibres, tactile textures and embroidered motifs articulate contemporary narratives in powerful ways.

subversive stitching

With their rich history of instructing, educating and inspiring, needlework samplers are unique in their ability to communicate important values or offer sources of amusement. Samplers were first seen during the early Renaissance in the convents and courts of Europe, where they were an integral part of women's education. As girls learned to stitch letters, numbers, biblical verses, moral maxims and pictorial elements, they developed needlework skills necessary for a future of domestic duties.

Few records document the roles of western women as well as these intricately-stitched samplers. Some of those made between the second half of the seventeenth century and the first half of the nineteenth century are especially interesting to art historians today. As historians identify vestiges of imagination, memory and emotion in the samplers, traditionally tropes ascribed to fine art, their parallels with the artworks of the period become more apparent.

Digital technology provides textile practitioners with innovative processes that liberate them from tedious, repetitive stitching, yet many artists prefer the homespun

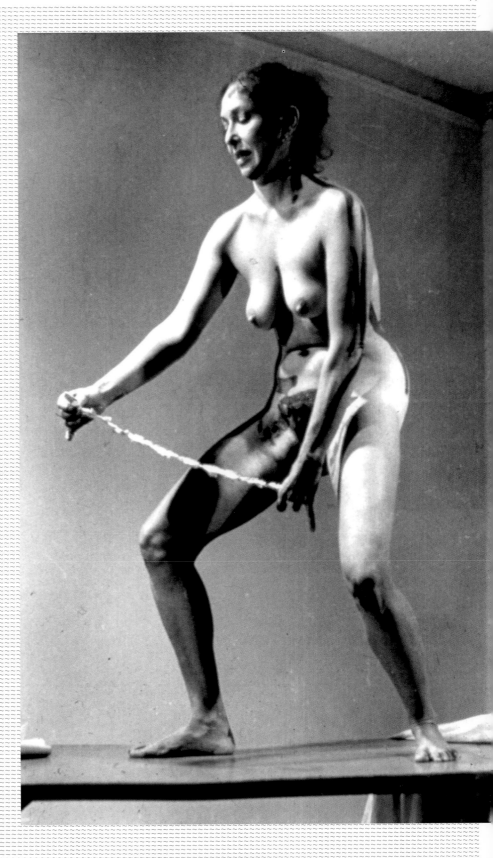

Carolee Schneemann, *Interior Scroll*, 1975.
Performance photograph. Image courtesy of Carolee Schneemann. Photo: Anthony McCall

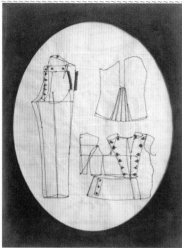

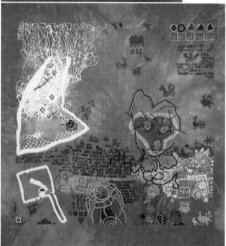

TOP TO BOTTOM

Annet Couwenberg, *Legs, Arms and Stomach*, 2001.
Based on a fable by Jean La Fontaine, 1621–1695. Digitised embroidery, flock,
dressmaking patterns in shadowbox, 39 x 31x 30 cm. Photo: Dan Meyers Photography.

Tilleke Schwarz, *Rites*, 2001.
Hand-embroidery, silk cotton and rayon yarn on linen cloth, pieces of material, lace and
textile paint, 67 x 74 cm.

Andrea Dezsö, *Lessons from my Mother*.
Embroidery, various threads on white cotton canvas. Image courtesy of the artist.

appeal of hand-crafted textiles. Dutch artist Annet Couwenberg merges both processes in works created through a method she describes as digitised embroidery. Repetition is a theme in Couwenberg's work, and digital technology enables her to repeat a single motif in different sizes, stitch patterns, orientations and palettes. Couwenberg cites seventeenth century Dutch samplers as an inspiration behind some of her work, rooting them in the tradition of creating popular motifs or precisely-stitched ciphers that are easy to identify and decode. As digital scans outline a precise pattern for Couwenberg to work from, she rejects their regularity by making random stitches or incorporating unexpected materials into her work.

Also from The Netherlands, Tilleke Schwarz finds inspiration in traditional samplers, which she updates with graphic elements found in graffiti, texts, icons and imagery. Schwarz' embroideries feature narrative elements rooted in the tradition of storytelling. But unlike the historical accounts ascribed to the annals of history, Schwarz' narratives rarely include a beginning, end, or even a storyline. As she deploys a narrative structure, viewers are invited to decode their meanings or imagine the connections between them. Schwarz relies on the viewer to complete the work; as she launches open-ended narratives, she deliberately lets go of conventional notions of authorship.

Andrea Deszö is a radical revisionist. As she revisits the traditional samplers of her native Transylvania, she rewrites the social and moral narratives that their surfaces usually depict. During her childhood, Deszö had been taught to follow the lessons that the samplers gave so that she would become a good wife and housekeeper one day. As she embroiders samplers today, she relays the other lessons she was taught as a young girl: "A women's legs are so strong that no man can spread them if she doesn't let him", "My mother claimed that men will like me more if I pretend to be less smart" and "My mother claimed that if you let a man fuck you he will leave you because every man wants to marry a virgin." By updating and reinventing Transylvanian samplers, Deszö rejects the 'wisdom' that these textiles once espoused.

Anila Rubiku is Albanian but lives in Italy, where she combines needlework with artificial light to create luminous textiles. Using techniques based on traditional Albanian embroidery, she stitches images depicting her travels between Milan and Tokyo across 50 linen surfaces fastened within wooden embroidery frames. Rather than document the journey with photography or video, Rubiku chose to record the experiences in a textile archive. Rubiku also constructs fabric sculptures in the shape of miniature houses and embellishes their surfaces with scenes of the domestic tasks traditionally carried out inside. As she uses the craft practice to evoke the experience of domesticity, she brings the private world of family life under public scrutiny.

Embroidery engages with three-dimensional space in the work of Xiang Yang, a political activist and artist from Beijing who immigrated to America. Yang has been producing contemporary art based on social and political themes from the very start of his career. During the Tiananmen Square protests, he was arrested when his cynical portrait of Mao Zedong was discovered. These days, Yang is best known for clashing images of disparate political leaders, such as Sadaam Hussein and George Bush, by embroidering their portraits onto clear plastic. Placing them back-to-back, with one a short distance behind the other, Xiang Yang pulls the threads from one embroidery to the other and back again as he stitches the images. The process results in long tubes of coloured threads stretching across the space between the two leaders, hinting at complicity between them.

Yang's unique work was sparked by experiments to transform a two-dimensional image into a three-dimensional shape. He had conceived of 'floating objects' that would take shape in empty space as sculptural forms. Although Yang had never tried needlework before, colourful silk thread and embroidery seemed to be the ideal material and methodology for building up sculptural images. Once he found a needle strong enough to pierce plastic, he practised creating picture-perfect likenesses of his subjects. Because he uses tensile thread to bridge two points some distance away from each other, Yang has to be careful to maintain the thread tension between the two images throughout their creation. Otherwise, the threads will sag when the images are set in place.

Born in The Netherlands but based in London, Michael Raedecker studied fashion design and fine art in Amsterdam. His trademark combination of painting and

TOP LEFT TO RIGHT

Anila Rubiku, *Houses of the Rising Sun*, 2005.
Sewn and perforated paper. Image courtesy Galerie Anita Beckers, Frankfurt.

Anila Rubiku, *Houses of the Rising Sun*, 2005.
Sewn and perforated paper. Image courtesy Galerie Anita Beckers, Frankfurt.

BOTTOM

Xian-Yang, *The Truth that People Are Not Willing to Face (Bushism vs Saddamism)*, 2006.
Thread, silk-screen, steel, 25.4 x 35.6 x 228.6 cm. Photo: Mei Lin.

Women war workers make knitted woolen jackets to cover the glass flasks of number 74 grenades (commonly known as "sticky bombs") at a factory workshop in Britain. The women, including Mrs. B. Colman (nearest to the camera) and Miss H. Brearley (center), fasten the jackets by means of a drawstring around the neck of the flask. The woolen jackets will soon be coated with adhesive to enable them to stick to their target before detonation. 1943.
Courtesy the Imperial War Museum, London.

Sabrina Gschwandtner, *Wartime Knitting Circle*, 2007.
Installation, machine-knitted acrylic wool, tablecloth, table, four stools, yarn, knitting needles, dimensions variable. Photo: Sabrina Gschwandtner.

embroidery has created a unique niche, and perhaps even a new genre of painting. Raedecker's work depicts classical subjects such as landscapes, portraits, interiors and still-lives, which he renders through unconventional methods. Sticky puddles of paint, tangled threads of yarn and intricately-stitched details use offbeat expressions to create a surreal sense of space. Layers of thread may be stitched over a collaged interior, which seem to radiate with the inner light of a glowing television screen.

Traditionally, painting is a practice that maintains a critical distance between the artwork and the spectator, but the agency of embroidery enables Raedecker to transcribe the epic into the personal. Because Raedecker incorporates craft fibres and techniques into his works, they become characterised by an unlikely intimacy that draws the viewer closer. Yet embroidery, as a solitary craft, also evokes a sense of emotional isolation. Rather than building lasting bridges between textile practice and art, it can also present an eerie sense of dislocation and unease.

East meets west in the work of Ke-Sook Lee, an artist who also combines painting with embroidery. Born in Korea, Lee studied applied arts in Soul before pursing post graduate painting studies in America. Lee's work explores the connections between traditional needlework and feminism, using thread to depict the fears, anxieties and hopes that have united Korean women for many generations. Lee has chosen to rely on images rather than words; aware that most women in her maternal ancestor's generations were illiterate, she uses embroidery to express her inspirations, just as they themselves would have done. Works such as *One Hundred Faceless Women* use vintage handkerchiefs and embroidery techniques to tell poignant stories of the female experience. Lee's works depict personal symbols from her own female experiences alongside symbols intended to represent universal womanhood. "Mirroring my inner self, my work continues to explore the boundaries of drawing", she said. "It evolves with stitching and embroidery to create a new kind of drawing that could hold my identity and experiences from my life in America as well as in Korea."[1]

revolutionary motifs

Needlework has a revolutionary past. It was used as a symbol of dissent by William Morris—one of the founders of the Arts and Crafts Movement—in his protest against industrial production. So that his work could continue to be produced by hand, Morris defied industrialists to support the Royal School of Needlework and single-handedly revitalised the art of tapestry-weaving in Britain. A similar rebellion was sparked a century later when feminist artists incorporated embroidery into their artwork. They challenged the distinction between art and craft that separated fibre art and fine art. Because needlework was considered to be a hobby or a domestic skill, the presence of sewn objects, needlepoint and samplers in art provoked the American art establishment. Needlework was eventually legitimated as an art form, but for several decades, stitched surfaces and sewn textiles continued to rank below the arts of painting and sculpture. Today's generation of emerging artists look to textiles as a source of innovation more than as a means of political dissent or radical rebellion. Fibres imbue artworks with texture and tactility, and incorporate craft practices that provide a means of creating radical expressions, subversive imagery, or simply beautiful motifs.

Sabrina Gschwandtner is an artist based in New York who works with film, video, photography, performance, sewing, crochet and knitting. In 2007, Gschwandtner created an interactive installation for the Museum of Arts and Design's exhibition *Radical Lace and Subversive Knitting* titled *Wartime Knitting Circle*, which consisted of nine machine-knitted photo blankets. Gschwandtner gathered images from newspapers, historical societies and library archives that depicted how knitting had been used during wartime for civic participation, protest, and more recently, as a popular way for families to remember relatives who had been deployed to Iraq and Afghanistan.

In an earlier work titled *Phototactic Behavior in Sewn Slides*, Gschwandtner stitched threads onto slides she had taken previously. When she projected the slides, the projector's fan blew the threads randomly, causing its automatic focusing mechanism to fluctuate wildly as it tried to focus on the threads attached to either side of the slides. The movements of the threads created an expression Gschwandtner likened to random animation, and the holes made by the sewing needle created a pattern when they were projected.

Ke-Sook Lee, *One Hundred Faceless Women*, detail, 2007. Hand-embroidery, pigment on a hundred vintage handkerchiefs, dimensions variable. Collection of the artist. Image courtesy George Billis Gallery, New York. © 2008 Ke-Sook Lee.

Ghada Amer, *The Definition of the Word Fear in English, French and Arabic,* 2007.
Acrylic and embroidery on canvas, 50.8 x 50.8 cm. © Amer 2007. Image courtesy of
Gagosian Gallery.

Ana de la Cueva, *Mending Traces*, 2007.
Digital print and embroidery with resin, 117 x 78 cm.

Ana de la Cueva is a Mexican artist who lives and works in New York. De la Cueva uses photography, video and mixed media to address issues of family traces, nomadic wanderings and migration. In works such as *Mending Traces*, de la Cueva uses paint to capture movement on paper, then digitally transfers the image onto linen. The fabric is sent to Mexican 'maquiladora' workshops along the Mexican-American border, where they are embroidered.[2] The resulting works effect portraits based on the direct involvement of the subject, who like a conventional 'sitter', posed for the portrait. De la Cueva incorporates geographical maps and graphic elements related to the subject's individual experience, resulting in what the artist describes as "stitched personal topographies".[3]

De la Cueva's works merge the personal experience of the individual with the political forces that shape it. Her video *Maquila* reveals the harsh repercussions of American legislation passed in 2006 that tightened measures to prevent illegal immigrants from passing the Mexican-American border. Many would-be émigrés rejected at the border end up working in one of the many maquiladoras located in local towns, where they produce textiles and a range of other products for American manufacturers. Paradoxically, this system serves the American economy much better than culling a low-paid labour force internally, because in Mexico, American industrialists are not legally obliged to maintain satisfactory working conditions, as they would be in the America.

Ghada Amer was born in Cairo and studied painting in France, but today, she lives and works in New York. Many of Amer's hand-embroidered paintings, with their intricately-stitched strands and delicate hanging threads, depict erotic abstractions. Her methodology defies the conventions of fine art and textile practice, and also refutes the norms of representing the female body in western art and Islamic culture. Amer's work deliberately challenges the role that needlework that has played in feminist art for the past three decades. By using needlework to create erotic images of the female body, and repeating the images serially as if to suggest a pattern, Amer shifts focus from feminism to eroticism, forging disconcerting alliances among feminist, Islamic, and postcolonial ideologies. Some of Amer's artworks embroider richly-coloured satin with translations of texts taken from the Qur'an. By translating the Arabic verses into French, Amer intended to create an obstacle that blocks English and Arabic-speaker's understanding of the original meanings. Works such as *The Definition of the Word Fear in English, French and Arabic* stitched phrases across the canvas and left threads hanging, as if to suggest that their narratives are ambiguous or incomplete. The three languages reflect the three cultures that Amer moves between, and also reference the Islamic-western political angst that she has experienced from several sides of the conflict.

Korean artist Cha Younwoo lived with the Tukano Indians of the Amazon for more than half a year, where he learnt the craft of weaving. During that time, Younwoo mastered the patterns and techniques shared by more than 400 tribes in the Amazon. Although they have similar ways of life, all of them speak different languages, and the cultural distinctions between them are often markedly different. Despite their differences, Younwoo discovered that their methods of weaving local materials were identical, and that the practice of weaving was one of the few traditions common to all the tribes.

As Younwoo learnt how to weave, he has also developed a range of other essential skills taught to the weavers of the Amazon. Younwoo learnt how to harvest the aroma plant and extract the reed-like fibres used in weaving, and how to handle the 'cipo', a rudimentary wooden tool that binds the fibres. When he returned home to southern California, Younwoo made a radical shift in his art practice. Rather than returning to the multi-media techniques and materials he had been working with previously, Younwoo decided to forge a fresh direction and use his newly-acquired craft skills to create woven portraits. In doing so, Younwoo has reinvented the modern portrait, a symbol of high culture, through the craft methodology of a primitive weaving technique. As an art medium, Younwoo describes weaving as "a natural process, very sustainable and eco-friendly" and considers the portrait to be "part of the native weaving work's twenty-first century evolution".[4]

Today, Younwoo's woven works form a bridge between western and indigenous cultures. His work enables Indian techniques to be valued as art methodology, and when he returns to the Amazon to teach the tribes how to weave contemporary textiles, the natives learn to use local materials and traditional techniques to create a commodity that boosts their economy. "I'm not approaching this with

a personal need to say 'this is art' and it needs to taught to indigenous peoples", he said. "I'm helping them understand that their craft can achieve new standards within their own culture, and that they can benefit from that in many different ways. They should be proud of that."

German artist Olaf Nicolai was also inspired by Brazilian textiles. A trip to Brazil led to Nicolai's first textile works. *Itamaraty* was a series of rugs sparked by the hand-woven textiles crafted by Aboriginal people in northern Brazil. Nicolai's versions were produced in the German town of Chemnitz, then exhibited at the Goethe-Institute in São Paulo. Nicolai produced another textile work based on the Bulgarian folk motif known as the *Peacock's Eye*, which he saw inscribed in ceramic objects in Bulgaria. In the spirit of Fernand Léger, who fused art with fabric design when he created a curtain for a skating rink in 1922, Nicolai's *Yeux de Paon*, a woven silk and cotton curtain, forms part of an ongoing experiment that rearticulates cultural models and ways of seeing.

Mattia Bonetti is a Paris-based Swiss designer who incorporates craft practices and art sensibilities into his designs. Over the years, Bonetti's work has featured a wide range of textile techniques, famously using embroidery to create a patchwork pattern for a sofa. Bonetti used pages torn from French publications and Chinese magazines, which he collaged together to create a single surface. The process of embroidering the finished fabric in a Chinese workshop was time-consuming and laborious, subsequently ensuring that the textile would sustain long-term wear and tear. The robust material that resulted contrasts sharply with the short-lived trends depicted in the media images that inspired the motifs.

Bonetti, and his partner Elizabeth Garouste, have previously created interior designs for French couture houses such as Christian Lacroix. "We want to produce furniture in the way a fashion collection is designed—like an idea, a desire", Garouste explained.[5] Their decision to use an embroidery technique in their contemporary design work reveals how influential couture practices are becoming in art and design, especially in places like Paris where the fashion industry influences many aspects of visual culture.

deconstructed fibres

The unspoken assumption of all textile practice is that it results in a 'finished' product. Yet, as artists find inspiration in textiles, they continually question this principle. Exploring whether a textile, like an art object, can ever be considered wholly complete, artists reveal that new methods of construction and consumption are changing traditional textile forms.

Deconstruction is both a philosophy and an aesthetic, and sometimes a metaphor for the dilapidation and disintegration associated with urban decay. It is poetically expressed in literature, film and philosophy, and is beautifully evident in iconic buildings such as Centre Pompidou in Paris, as well as in the shredded chic of Martin Margiela's garments. The artistic equivalent of such deconstructed forms is probably the shredded canvases created by Stefan Müller, an artist based in Berlin. Müller is known for exploring Reductivist aesthetics, and most of his artworks deconstruct painting to the bare essentials. Müller typically presents large expanses of empty, unprimed raw canvas, sparsely traced with pigments or dye, or sometimes bleached to create a variety of shades and tones through the use of a single material. Among Müller's most radical paintings are the untitled works comprised of strips of shredded linen woven into a painterly surface. By using the stretcher strips as a loom and winding a warp of torn canvas lengths from top to bottom, Müller threads a weft of shredded canvas through his 'loom'. The effect is that of a woven artwork, where torn selvedges and hanging threads create a richly textured surface. Like Lucio Fontana's slashed canvases, perforations in the paintings' surfaces give them an unexpected dimension and invert traditional understandings of the division between the visible and the unseen.

Contrasting sharply with many of his German contemporaries, Müller's formal characteristics are closely aligned with post-Minimalism and the Colour Field painting movement, although neither of those labels encompass the methodology he uses. Although fabric traditionally underpins most paintings, neither art theory nor professional art practice have a vocabulary that articulates the role that textiles play today.

TOP TO BOTTOM

Olaf Nicolai, *Yeux de Paon*, 2007.
Woven silk and cotton, 350 x 800 cm. Published by Carolina Nitsch Contemporary Art, New York.

Stefan Müller, *Untitled*, 2005.
Various tissues applied on tissue, 130 x 270 cm. Image courtesy of Galerie Bärbel Grässlin, Frankfurt aM. Photo: Wolfgang Günzel, Offenbach Am.

Moira Chester is a London-based sculptor who uses recycled materials, particularly fabrics, to create deconstructed garments. Translucent 'dresses' are sewn from reclaimed textiles, scaffolding scrim, paper, plastic and metal, or stitched together by using pins, nails or wire. Although Chester's garments are sculptures, their aesthetic links them to the deconstructed fashion aesthetic pioneered by designers such as Hussein Chalayan, Robert Cary-Williams and Junya Watanabe, whose shredded fabrics, unconventional materials and rudimentary construction processes once mirrored contemporary art more than fashion.

French Anthropologist Claude Lévi-Strauss would have been fascinated by the methodologies Chester employs, since he explored the significance of production-oriented activities that do not rely upon traditional materials or methods to produce form.[6] Terming the process 'bricolage', Lévi-Strauss described activities such as fashioning doll dresses from scraps of fabrics and pieces of string, or transforming lint, fluff and felt into tiny sculptures. Lévi-Strauss's model of bricolage extends beyond these analogies to address both methods of garment production, and art forms. As Chester engages with unconventional materials and non-traditional techniques, her work displays a basic form of creativity that refutes the myth that high art should result from conventional processes. Chester's departure from pre-established methodology, like those of radical fashion designers, challenges preconceived views of fashion textiles, art materials, and the roles of the makers who create with them.

Most of Louise Bourgeois' works are more likely to be interpreted in terms of Abstract Expressionism or American High Modernism than they are as deconstructed textile forms. For most of her career, Bourgeois has investigated the masculine persona of Expressionism through robust works cast in bronze, wood and stone. But relatively late in her career, Bourgeois turned to textile forms as means of representing simple things, often ripping the textiles apart, shredding them, and joining them together with Frankenstein-like stitching. The child of parents who owned a tapestry workshop, Bourgeois is well-versed in textile production and techniques. Bourgeois' textile works create a nexus of making, wearing, dwelling and thinking about the meaning of fabric.

Fibres, whether spun by spiders or created on a spinning wheel, have deep significance for Bourgeois, who says that threads weave important memories and emotional connections for us all. Threads become cloth, and the significance of ripped surfaces, torn selvedges and roughly-sewn seams in her work reflect the emotional turmoil that childhood memories have for Bourgeois. As she deconstructs the textiles to basic forms, she intentionally subverts the soothing tranquility traditionally associated with textiles. Ultimately, for Bourgeois, textiles are loaded with feelings of responsibility, vulnerability and anxiety, as much for her today as when she was a child.

A work that encapsulates these tensions most strongly is the untitled fabric and steel sculpture Bourgeois produced in 1998. The sculpture is a woman's torso crafted in a metal structure resembling the components of an old-fashioned box-spring mattress. Virtually transparent, the sheer nylon stretched over it enables the viewer to see all parts of the sculpture, subsequently bringing to mind a vessel more than a physical body. Yet a bulbous, pregnant, padded form attached to the sculpture's lower abdomen remains opaque. The nylon is ragged at the seams and brutally sewn together in areas representing the genitals and the neck. Other textile sculptures made by Bourgeois around this time are stitched together seamlessly, but here, her deconstructed approach to both fabric and sewing technique clearly articulate the tensions that Bourgeois invests in these areas of the body.

In 2007, Bourgeois produced *The Passage* and *Woven Child,* two textile-based works. Bourgeois explored the physical and psychological aspects of being both mother and child. Both works depict a graphic outline of a pregnant women, her foetus clearly visible in the womb. Each is drawn in an intense blue pigment. The maternal figure in *The Passage* dominates the work, while the figure in *Woven Child* is virtually eclipsed by a textile of woven ribbons. The absent child is brutally shrouded within the woven form, as if to suggest burial. But coupled with the depiction of the unborn foetus beside it, the loose, unfinished construction of the textile form represents an object that is still in the process of being formed. Weaving, as a basic textile process and one that traditionally produces a finished object, provides a poignant metaphor for the unborn child.

Moira Chester, *Nail Dress*, 2003–2004.
Scrim and nails, 119.4 x 48.3 x 7.3 cm.

seamless space

Exciting exchanges are taking place between textiles and space. Their fascination for one another seems to spiral around their mutual desire to see space transmuted into art. As contemporary artists explore a textile's tactile allure, they discover its intrinsic ability to demarcate space, absorb sound, and create decorative elements that combine the poetics of art with the aesthetic features of design.

American artist Piper Shepard is opening new dialogues between art and architecture as her art practice incorporates three-dimensional construction techniques as well as interventions in space. Despite their architectonic characteristics, Shepard's creations are some of the most delicate hand-made textiles seen in contemporary art today. Although Shepard relies on traditional processes such as sewing, cutting, printing, etching and dyeing, the textiles that result are unconventional in proportion and design. Shepard's work has the delicacy of the fine-boned patterns characteristic of lace and is often mistaken for it. Unlike a traditional lace practitioner, she doesn't rely on bobbins, threads, pricking cards and needlelace pillows to create her textiles, rather she coats long lengths of cotton muslin with graphite, then hand-cuts an exquisite, intricate lace pattern into the fabric. Once hung in place and spectacularly lit, the panels taint their surroundings with the elaborate shadows they cast.

Simple in shape and elegant in design, the lace-like panels Shepard creates are architectural in scale, and hang from the ceiling to create architectonic enclosures. Both sides of the work are visible at once, appearing to be both skin and bone, inside and outside, and their surfaces seem interchangeable. Although they construct small monuments to architecture they are big testaments to the intricate textile techniques. They also provide elegant reminders of textiles' long history, harkening back to a time when textile tents provided domestic enclosures, and fabric panels were battened to the walls as a source of insulation and decor. Shepard's unique work is also forging new directions for architectonic textiles. In collaboration with a manufacturer of architectural components, Shepard has designed motifs for a system of architectural panels coated in transparent resin. Her textiles bring poetry to function, creating architectural artefacts as a result.

With their sculptural silhouettes, minimalist motifs and textured surfaces, the fabrics designed by Finnish-born artist Anne Kyyrö Quinn are currently some of the most visionary expressions of felt textiles. One of the first contemporary artists to rediscover felt and update it for the twenty-first century, Quinn broke fresh ground when she used the material to pioneer a striking range of interior textiles. An arts graduate, Quinn combines her art training with her design skills to create richly textured textile panels. Inspired by the felt structures crafted by artists such as Joseph Beuys and Eva Hesse, Quinn eschews surface embellishment to expose the substance, structure and tactility that woolen felt has. Exhibited at the Royal Academy in London and at the Haute Green design gallery in New York, Quinn's works move easily between art and design.

When Quinn's art panels were spotted by an architect, she was offered several public commissions, most famously at the National Tennis Centre in Wimbledon, where she designed large-scale installations in felt. "Working in an architectural way enabled me to find new expressions for my artistic skills, even some as commercial applications", she said.[7] Because felt is a sound-absorbent material, and Quinn's work is so richly textured, ambient sound actually transformed her art panels into acoustic 'sponges' that soak up noise. Regarded as a unique example of sound-absorbent art, Quinn's textile panels are in demand by leading architects and interior designers.

Janet Echelman is an American artist who uses fibres to shape and define architectural space. Through her art, Echelman redefines urban spaces with monumental public sculptures made of diaphanous, flexible nets that move and change shape with the elements. All of her commissions are site-specific, and many of her sculptural installations are built outdoors, where they are designed to interact with natural forces such as wind and water. Because the nature of her work requires materials that allow air currents to move through her sculptures—a feature of her work that she describes as 'wind choreography'—Echelman discovered that strong fibres and lightweight fabrics are ideal materials for her art. Light also plays an important role in her work; rays of sunlight cast light and shadows over

TOP

Piper Shepard, *Chambers*, 2002.
Installation view at The Baltimore Museum of Art, 2005, hand-cut muslin, ink, gesso, steel armatures, five panels, each 2.7m x 119.4 cm x 45.7 cm.

BOTTOM

Anne Kyyro Quinn, *Leaf Wall Panel*, 2003.
100 per cent wool felt. Photo: Rachel Jones.

Janet Echelman, *She Changes*, 2005.
Waterfront plaza, Porto and Matosinhos, Portugal, Tenara® PTFE architectural fiber,
height 50 X 150 X 150 m. Image courtesy of Joao Ferrand and www.echelman.com.

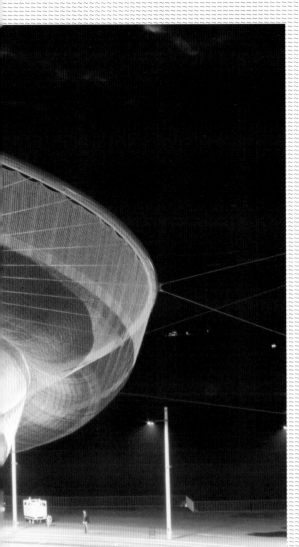

her sculptures by day, and by night, floodlights transform her work into glowing, luminous shapes. Echelman also considers how her sculptures project shadows onto adjoining surfaces, adding additional layers of movement and depth.

Echelman sky-rocketed to fame when she completed the extraordinary wind sculpture titled *She Changes,* built on the waterfront in Porto, Portugal in 2005. The sculpture was created in collaboration with a textile manufacturer, an architect and a software developer. "The artwork is actually a complex, multi-layered form created by twisting, braiding and knotting nearly one ton of Tenara® fibres", Echelman explained.[8] "I got help from Phillip Speranza, a New York-based architect, to translate my drawings into three-dimensional computer models, then asked Peter Heppel in Paris develop a software programme for the piece. The software showed me how the sculpture would move in the wind and revealed what engineering considerations there would be." The textile structure was fabricated in Washington State by hand and by machine, then shipped to Portugal in pieces. Cranes were brought to the site to hang it, where it was suspended from a massive ring of hollow steel hung between three steel poles of varying heights. "The sculpture is similar to a net", Echelman explained. "It was created using a fibre that could withstand a windy environment with long periods of UV exposure. Tenara is light enough to respond to the wind and durable enough to retain its red pigment despite long periods of UV exposure. I had looked at plant fibres, silk and nylon, but none of them have the durability of Tenara."

Dave Cole, an American artist based in Providence, Rhode Island, takes knitting to new heights by creating extreme textiles that reach proportions never before thought possible. Cole is a sculptor who discovered knitting while he was a visual arts student at Brown University. "I've been knitting my art work for a number of years now and I'm always trying to make things on a larger scale", Cole explained. "I want to push boundaries and see what's possible in knitting, and so far, I haven't found anything that proved to be impossible."[9]

Cole's knitted projects began with robust works, which he produced in small scales that he could create with conventional techniques. Those works typically explored the tenderness of childhood and the brutality of grown-up violence. For example, Cole knitted an unwearable baby blanket out of spun silica, a fibre so durable it can withstand temperatures above melting point. He also knitted a jumper from Kevlar webbing, a material strong enough to stop bullets and hoist lorries into the air, and crafted robust teddy bears from sheets of metal, which he had cut into thin strips and then knitted it into a teddy bear shape.

Cole decided to create another non-tactile teddy bear by knitting it out of fibreglass insulation. Commissioned by the Decordova Museum of Contemporary Art and constructed on-site, the teddy bear measured more than four metres high and was nearly six metres wide. Cole created the bear by bending and looping the fibreglass strips into knit stitches by hand. Although he wore gloves and an industrial Tyvek protection suit, friction from the fibreglass cut through his protective clothing and came in contact with his skin. "It was an itchy experience", Cole remembered. "To knit the teddy bear's belly, I had to jump inside it and push the stitches out. That created friction between the suit and the fibreglass that wore holes in the tyvek."

In 2002, on the first anniversary of 9/11, Cole created a giant American flag to memorialise the event. Commissioned by city officials in Provincetown, Cole attached five metre long aluminium posts to the mechanical arms of two John Deere excavators. The lamp posts served as knitting needles, and the excavators provided the power to lift them into the air and manoeuvre them in knitting strokes. Cole stood on a boom suspended over the 'knitting needles', and using a long fishing rod dubbed 'the crochet hook', he fed 30 centimetre wide strips of felt into the 'needles' below. By the time he was finished, Cole had created an American flag that was more than four metres wide. Although the flag was commissioned as a public artwork, it was laden with personal memories and emotions of Cole's own experiences following the 9/11 attacks in New York. "I spent the week after the attacks in New York where I volunteered to do search-and-rescue work", Cole said. "At the time, I felt like I'd never be able to get my head around what had happened. So I went down to New York to get my hands around it. That's how I understand things."

Jim Drain, another American artist with links to Providence and an interest in knitted textiles, also creates fabric forms for three-dimensional spaces. After graduating from the Rhode Island School of Design in 1998, Drain used a knitting machine for the first time and discovered a new direction for his art

Dave Cole, *Decordova Teddy Bear,* 2004.
Fiberglass insulation, 40 x 40 x 35 cm. Decordova Museum of Contemporary Art.

Jim Drain, *AIDS-a-delic*, 2005.
Mixed media with yarn, fabric, and beads, 213.4 x 152.4 x 101.6 cm. Image courtesy of Greene Naftali, New York.

practice. The knitted objects he produced perfectly expressed the messages he wanted to communicate: hard narratives cocooned in soft textures.

Since then, Drain has become respected as a mixed media artist who typically coats the surfaces of his works with yarn, fabric and beads. His choice of materials is often described as 'gaudy' by American critics: silver fringe, strings of brightly-coloured plastic beads and terry cloth bath towels depicting images of a bare-breasted women have embellished several of his installations. Drain's installations use textile forms to explore how identities can be created, dissolved and formulated anew. Drain's use of fibres, appliqué, and embroidery embellishments, together with some of the 'trashy' elements of mainstream American tastes, form his critique of America's consumerist, celebrity-crazed culture. His works are rooted in the everyday and the ordinary, proposing a rhetoric of communication through social space. The installations use the space around them to alter our relationships to each other and to ourselves, exploring the impact of materials, colour, tactility and tropes of memory to create places which are at once real and imagined. Such sensual devices are also common to architecture, where, likewise, they highlight the gulf between private experience and public content.

From his base in New York, multi media artist Bayard—who goes by only one name—also crafts installations using textile materials and methodologies. Although Bayard is an acclaimed artist, his artistic range is not limited to visual art; he is also an author with more than 150 short stories published worldwide. Bayard also founded the avant-garde literary journal, *Happy*. Although he is comfortable articulating the narratives underpinning his works, he is also passionate in his belief that art should speak for itself without having to bear the burden of interpretation or make declarations of meaning. His works are intended to be accessible and immediate, drawing the viewer in and encouraging them to interact and interpret the works in any way they choose.

Bayard artworks give textiles a platform to express themselves in a sculptural guise. His sculptures are eye-catching and intriguing; ranging from small, intimate pieces to installations made on a monumental scale, they typically combine three different textile forms. Mohair yarn is delicately wound through a wooden frame to create hanging installations, while silicon-coated rip-stop nylon and coloured threads are combined with non-woven fabrics to craft inflatable sculptures. Textiles, foam rubber and rhinestones are bound with acrylic yarn to construct his bellicose foam 'poems'. Many of his works are site-specific, and his diverse styles and different locations are united by his consistent use of fibres and his vibrant sense of colour, creating tactile forms. Bayard's works create a momentary pause in a high-speed world.

Lucy Orta is an artist who refutes the idea that textiles and built environments are separate entities. With art as her medium, her work examines the axis between textiles and buildings, reclaiming both of them as sculptural, tactile and architectural expressions of society. As Orta's wearable shelters critique social and political issues, they also provide practical solutions to the problems of transitional living. There are reportedly five hundred million homeless people around the world, and the garment-cum-shelters Orta creates provides a potent response to the practical problems of every one of them. Through a series of installations, exhibitions and social interventions that put her textile structures to practical use, Orta has consistently addressed the social conditions that condemn individuals to an existence on the margins of society.

Orta's point of departure from conventional art was her use of textiles to produce and define urban space, conceptually as well as materially. Recognising textiles' potential to soothe separateness and foster belonging, Orta used it to designate separate spheres and collective worlds for temporary habitation. Orta initially created a series of waterproof garments known as *Refuge Wear* that transform into basic tent structures to provide shelter for homeless individuals. She later created garments known as *Nexus Architecture* that zip together to unite several people in a literal and symbolic link. These structures amplify fabric's inherent power to communicate, negotiate social bonds and unite members of a community. Orta's work centres around the ephemeral nature of these social bonds, tracing their networks within the systems of habitation that create community and a sense of belonging.

Orta uses textiles to relate the story of the tension between movement and stillness, between the visible and the invisible. Orta describes the plight of the urban homeless today as "tangible invisibility" but finds them ever-present. She follows their traces as they "literally melt and disappear into the margins and framework

TOP

Bayard, *Amos And Icarus*, 2007.
Silicone impregnated rip stop nylon, thread fan, 182 x 222.8 x 228 cm.

BOTTOM

Bayard, *The Seven Sisters*, 2006–2007.
Mohair and wood, 12 units, 670 x 18 x 18 cm each.

of the city", combating their "disappearance" by rendering the invisible visible once more. Combining the vocabularies of art, fashion and architecture, Orta harnesses the visual power they all project: "From a design perspective, seeing a suit that can transform into a tent-like structure is visually very interesting. It brings awareness to the person inside it. As an artist, I define the visual aspects of the work to transmit a message from the wearer to onlookers or passers-by. Whether or not they have acknowledged the homeless before, they can no longer ignore them if they wear the pieces I designed."[10] Orta inscribes the fabrics with texts, symbols and images that mimic tattoos, packaging or urban graffiti. "There is an ongoing dialogue in my work between the principles of design, social awareness and concepts of visibility. It brings issues into view."

The concept of establishing a social network is developed more elaborately in Orta's *Modular Architecture* project, a forum she established to clothe, shelter and protect the wearers while joining them together to form a single, linked environment. Resembling flexible architectural components in their design, they merge the solidarity afforded by *Nexus Architecture* with the utility of *Refuge Wear*. Individuals can attach links to share and circulate body heat, or use the system of pockets and zippers to create a single survival shelter by fully integrating four individual pieces. The pockets also function as containers for storing food, water and supplies, with their shared design facilitating the circulation of resources. The garments-cum-habitats can be removed and assembled in the manner of modular architecture, reconnecting the inhabitants to a secure sense of belonging. "The physical link weaves the social link", Orta explained. "There is a sense that these communities include—and are constructed by—individual, intimate spaces that are united in a homogenous whole."

second skins

The growing symbiosis between textiles and art is generating a new body consciousness. Just as textiles play a key role in moulding the body's shape into stylised 'second skin' apparel or crafting rigid garments that define space around the body, they also lend themselves to the creation of sculptural shapes that explore new representations of the human form.

The body politic is a focal point for Chicago-based artist Nick Cave, who may be best known for his *Soundsuits*, the wearable sculptures constructed from found and recycled objects. Cave, who studied fibre art at the Cranbrook Academy of Art, is currently the chair of the fashion department at the Art Institute of Chicago. As the disciplines of art, textile design and fashion converge in his work, Cave's creations blur the boundaries between surface design, performance art, costume and social activism. When worn on the body, the *Soundsuits* are deployed as ritualistic costumes which Cave and other dancers wear for live performances and videos. Set up as gallery installations, they become extravagant showcases of otherworldly silhouettes that feature painted fabric, intricate jewellery and collages of reclaimed objects. Cave has said: "I believe that the familiar must move towards the fantastic. I want to evoke feelings that are unnamed, that aren't realised except in dreams."[11]

The suits' role in the performances—which Cave refers to as "ritualistic dance"—seems to connect them to African ceremonial costumes, while the labour-intensive, highly-skilled techniques used to construct them forge links to couture processes. Yet, flea market finds, such as plastic beads, fake flowers, costume jewellery and key chains, which transform the textiles into highly-seductive visual surfaces, imbue them with retro nostalgia and pop culture ciphers. Cave describes this aspect of his work as "the act of collecting and reconfiguring", a concept that brings contemporary art closer to the recycling ethos pioneered by textile practitioners such as Becky Earley and Luisa Cevese.[12] Cave's use of recycled materials has been likened to quilt-making, which fashions decorative and functional textiles from discarded cloth. Likewise, Cave reclaims worthless materials and transforms them into resplendent surfaces.

Cave's *Soundsuits* are literally larger than life; they almost cover the entire body, sometimes only revealing the eyes. Masking the wearer's identity is central to Cave's work. An African-American male, Cave claims that he encounters prejudice virtually every time he steps onto the street, and the *Soundsuits* provide a disguise that poetically thwarts the prejudices some African-Americans encounter. Some of the materials appliquéd onto the suits, such as twigs and bottle-caps, are discarded

Nick Cave, *Soundsuit*, 2005.
Cotton knits, fabricated appliqué surface, metal armature, found vintage metal flowers.

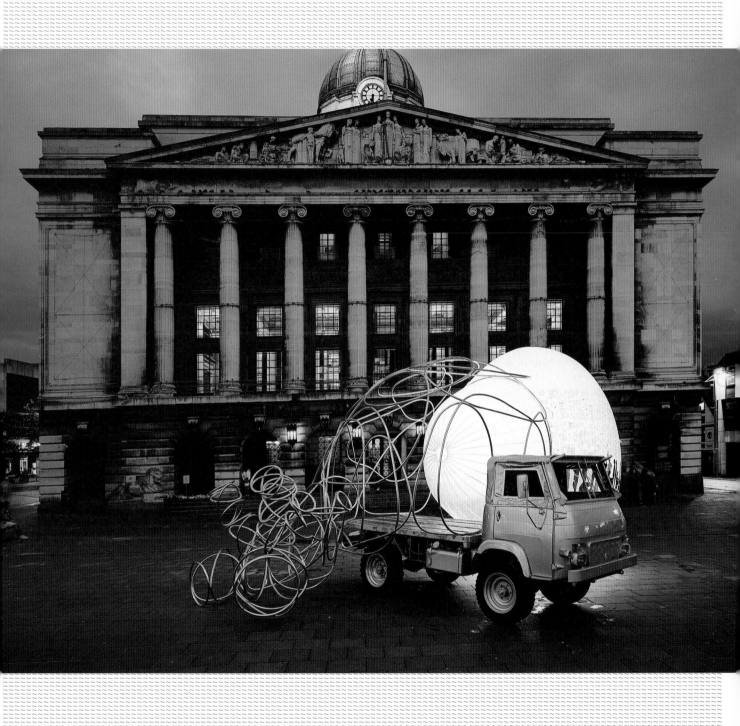

Lucy Orta, *Dwelling X* – Installation in Market Square, Nottingham, 2004.
Reconditioned army lorry, steel structure, inflatable, silk-screen print, pump. Curated by
Paula Orrell for Angel Row Gallery and Now festival.

Kristian Kozul, *Untitled (Boots)*, 2007.
Cowboy boots, sequins, tassels, spikes, 38 x 13 x 30 cm.

items that have little value. In Cave's eyes, they represent American society's view of African-American males. The *Soundsuits* are intended to summon something beyond skin itself, transcending the body within it as it takes the wearer to a space free of class, race or gender.

Although Cave examines personal identity from the perspective of his cultural background and racial makeup, he strives to create art that reflects some of the universal tropes that characterise human experience today. As such, parallels can be drawn between Cave's work and the art of the late Brazilian artists Lygia Clark and Hélio Oiticica, who examined the mutability of the body through its relationship to signifiers outside it. They created wearable structures for temporary 'habitation' in order to explore identity and personal space. The *Parangolés,* Oiticica's best-known works, were fabricated from textiles and plastics. Similar to Cave's work, the *Parangolés* were also commentaries on the individual's role in collective experience as, "a participant, transforming his own body into a prop, in a ludic experience that becomes an expressive act".[13]

Kristian Kozul is a German-born Croatian artist who lives in New York. Inspired by European and American folk traditions, Kozul transforms banal objects into outrageous artefacts. By combining craft techniques and couture practices, processes that are often at odds with mass-produced objects, Kozul creates fetishistic forms that transcend the item's original function. As Kozul takes elements of country and western culture, and lavishly embroiders them or stitches them with sequins, he creates new forms that question the underlying cultural and political assumptions associated with the original.

Kozul created his own version of a mechanical bull, which he dressed up in Las Vegas showgirl glamour. He embellished the saddle with shiny sequins and feathers, then embedded the leather portions with chrome spikes, giving it a masochistic undertone. The mechanical bull replaced the bucking stallions that American pioneers once learned to tame and train. Today, it symbolises 'taming the beast' in pop culture. Kozul was fascinated by the importance that a mechanical bull played in *Urban Cowboy,* the dramatic film starring John Travolta and Debra Winger.[14] The film portrayed the mechanical bull as a representation of 'lo-brow' culture, yet it was also charged with sexual undertones. Throughout the film, the mechanical bull was ridden by both men and women, generating a genderless signifier of sexuality. Kozul's take on the mechanical bull today acknowledges these roles by 'dressing' it in textile forms that evoke both masculinity and femininity. In this 'drag', the mechanical bull is no longer genderless, but a dual-gendered creature.

Kozul has also invoked symbols from country and western culture in other works. Taking traditional cowboy hats and cowboy boots as his starting point, he has crafted unwearable versions of these iconic garments covered in red, white, and blue sequins, trimming them in fringe and inlaying them with chrome spikes. Kozul used these objects in reference to another cultural character, the 'daredevil' performer, which he first discovered while watching televised repeats of American stuntman, Evel Knievel.[15] A daredevil willingly faces danger, and dares to attempt perilous feats, or take risks in exchange for personal gain. Kozul believes that such characters are unique to the American way of life, and is fascinated by how the daredevil merges national identity and personal pride with the demands of the entertainment industry. Kozul's choice of red, white and blue colours represent the daredevil's expression of national identity, while the shiny sequins and flamboyant fringes reference the performance aspects of the public events he daredevil staged.

Kozul creates other sculptures based on iconic imagery. The objects are often diverse, ranging from fabled forms, such as the horn of plenty, or functional items such as wheelchairs, walking sticks, and urinals. Such clinical forms are designed to be practical and efficient; beauty and aesthetics are seldom factored into the design processes. Through the agency of textiles and haberdashery, Kozul created his *Discoware* series of care objects exquisitely trimmed and decorated with items such as lace doilies, ribbons, feathers and beads, and embellished with rhinestones and pearls. The resulting forms are sumptuous objects, yet remain perfectly functional. At the same time, they continue to represent illness or disability, which they soothe beneath a surface of faux glamour.

Guerra de la Paz is the collective name that describes the creative duo of Cuban-born artists, Alain Guerra and Neraldo de la Paz. The two artists initially worked individually while sharing a studio in Miami, where they returned after studying in the mid-west. What initially began as a collaborative project has evolved into an ongoing body of work that spans more than a decade.

TOP TO BOTTOM

Kristian Kozul, *Untitled (saddle I),* 2007.
Saddle, sequins, feathers, spring, spikes, 109 x 71 x 71 cm.

Kristian Kozul, *Untitled (bull),* 2007.
Mechanical bull, sequins, spikes, feathers, bull: 178 x 165 x 63.5 cm, skirt: 4 m.

Their choice material today is the found object, and most of their work is constructed from reclaimed textiles that they have scavenged and sorted, deconstructed or incorporated whole. Lengths of textiles are categorised by colour and motif, then cut, shredded, sewn and wrapped into a range of familiar forms or otherworldly creations. In galleries and museums, they have reconstructed whole landscapes out of reclaimed textiles, or created installations from mounds of material carefully layered by colour. They believe that textiles, as a tactile art material, invite the viewer to experience the work more intimately through their remembered associations with fabrics in various forms.

The absent body is a feature of their figurative works. Guerra de la Paz construct life-sized 'families' from reclaimed cloth, which are rich in references and nuanced on many levels. The figures are ascribed the traditional roles of parents, grandparents and siblings, and remain true to typical body proportions. Gloves are used to suggest hands and folded textiles create facial features, while myriad layers are sculpted into bodily contours. Although the figures are stylised, gendered and ascribed an age range, their generic identities enables them to transcend notions of race or nationality. Body images like these are ground breaking in that they wholeheartedly reject the icon bodies of visual culture, which many of today's figurative artists portray in terms of the super-heroes of action films, sylph-like supermodels and surgically-enhanced pop stars.

Guerra de la Paz salvaged a number of neckties and transformed them into sculptural forms. Playing upon the neckties' role as a constricting object, they constructed nooses from them, or fashioned them into snakes poised to encircle their prey. Nooses and snakes are universal forms that are feared in many cultures, but replicated from colourful neckties, they become tactile objects that draw viewers closer rather than scaring them away.

From her studio in Washington, DC, Melissa Ichiuji crafts figurative sculptures from soft fibres and supple fabrics. Ichiuji draws upon her background as a dancer and actor to poise the figures in ways that suggest movement, or sit them in positions that represent physical pain or inner conflicts. "Each work begins with a personal association and then expands to address a more universal theme often having to do with fantasies relating to power, sexual awakening, repressed anger and violence, and feelings of loss and mortality", Ichiuji wrote. "My figures often appear to be at once infantile and ageing, both disconnected and active. They are struggling to make sense of the world and the conflicting messages found within it."[16]

Each figure is sewn and assembled using a combination of natural and synthetic materials such as latex, nylon, leather, fur and human hair. Although the sculptures' hand-made construction gives them the intimate quality of a craft object, many of them appear to be animal/human hybrids that summon a disturbing aesthetic. Part of the discomfort they instill may be due to their rejection of the wider social trends that shape and control contemporary bodies. Ichiuji's figures morph into diseased and decrepit shapes, bodies no longer controlled through surgical procedures or radical exercise. They refute the premise that a body's representations in visual culture should encourage us to believe that the body is the passport to all that is valued in life, that health, youth, beauty, sex and fitness are the hallmarks of an acceptable body image. Though, Ichiuji's figures are harmless, they are powerful theatres for the performances of some of life's most radical rituals.

The son of a painter and a puppeteer, Benji Whalen grew up among artists. From an early age, he was exposed to painterly motifs and miniature representations of the body, and both influences seem to characterise his work today. After gaining a masters degree in painting at the San Francisco Art Institute in 1997, Whalen discovered embroidery on a visit to his grandmother. He noticed that most of her interior textiles had been embellished with elaborate needlework. Whalen asked his mother to teach him basic embroidery stitches, and since then, he's been embroidering cloth, making dummies and creating textile-based installations as well as continuing to paint in oils.

Textiles began featuring in Whalen's work when he was still at university. "At the end of my first year, I began painting on printed fabrics", he said, in an interview with Ilana Stanger.

> It was a lot of fun to do. To come to stretched fabric and already have a buzzing visual field of print and to paint on top of that was pretty exhilarating. It's like putting butter on hot pan: as soon as you touch it, it's already operating on a hot field. Eventually I realised paint on fabric was kind of contrived... but paint wasn't an integral part of the material, paint was being imposed on it.[17]

TOP TO BOTTOM

Guerra de la Paz, *Family*, 2004.
Mixed media, Twenty-first century Museum Collection.

TOP

Melissa Ichiuji, *School Girl*, 2006.
Pantyhose, blocks, cotton and teeth, 25.4 x 61 x 50.8 cm. Photo: Brandon Webster.
Image courtesy of Irvine Contemporary.

BOTTOM

Melissa Ichiuji, *Garden Party*, 2006.
Fabric, human hair, latex and cotton, each figure approximately 75 x 25 x 30 cm.
Photo: Helmuth Humphrey. Image courtesy of Irvine Contemporary.

Whalen says that part of embroidery's appeal is that it creates unique surfaces that would be difficult to reproduce by hand and virtually impossible to reproduce mechanically. Whereas each human body is unique in its individuality and impossible to copy, it can be physically altered, cosmetically enhanced or surgically redefined. Tattooing is one means of enhancing the body with a unique motif that identifies it as an individual entity. Whalen considers tattooing to be a fascinating practice. Like embroidery, tattooing is needle-based, executed in a wide range of styles and designs. Because tattoos are such powerful ciphers, we commonly believe that they hold clues to knowing more about the individuals they are inscribed on.

Whalen reconstructs arms in fabrics, and embroiders tattoo motifs onto them. His 'tattoos' feature biker emblems, religious iconography, Goth symbols and sexual fantasies. They point out that our skin, like the surface of a textile, can be a compelling signifier of identity, and transmit powerful messages about those that it belongs to.

The works of these artists, like those of the previous sections, are pulling together some of the most exciting strands of contemporary visual culture today. Body empowerment, hybrid materials, radical new techniques and fresh interpretations of space suggest exciting new directions for both contemporary art and textile design. As new forms unfold, with them come groundbreaking materials, new functions and new roles for the textile-based practices of the future.

1. From www.georgebillis.com.
2. Maquiladoras are factories that import materials and equipment on a duty-free and tariff-free basis for assembly or manufacturing, they then export the assembled product.
3. From www.latincollector.com/exhibitions.
4. Cha Younwoo was interviewed by the author at Art Basel Miami, 2007.
5. Worthington, Christa, "The Importance of Being Whimsical", *The New York Times*, 18 October 1987.
6. Lévi-Strauss, Claude, *The Savage Mind*, Chicago: University of Chicago Press, 1968.
7. Anne Kyyrö Quinn was interviewed by the author.
8. Janet Echelman was interviewed by the author.
9. Dave Cole was interviewed by the author at Art Basel Miami in 2007.
10. Lucy Orta was interviewed by the author.
11. From www.jackshainman.com/dynamic/exhibit_artist.
12. For specific information on the sustainable work of these designers, see *Seamless* by Bradley Quinn, London: Laurence King, 2008.
13. Basualdo, Carlos, *Hélio Oiticica: Quasi-Cinemas*, Ostfildern-Ruit, Germany: Hatje Cantz Publishers, 2002, p. 140.
14. *Urban Cowboy* was directed by James Bridges and screened in 1980.
15. Evel Knievel was an American stuntman popular in the 1960s and 70s. Knievel typically attempted motorcycle jumps and often wore red, white and blue costumes embroidered with stars.
16. From www.melissaichiuji.com.
17. Interview quotes reprinted from New York Foundation for the Arts website www.nyfa.org. The artist was interviewed by Ilana Stanger of ArtBiz.com in 2007.

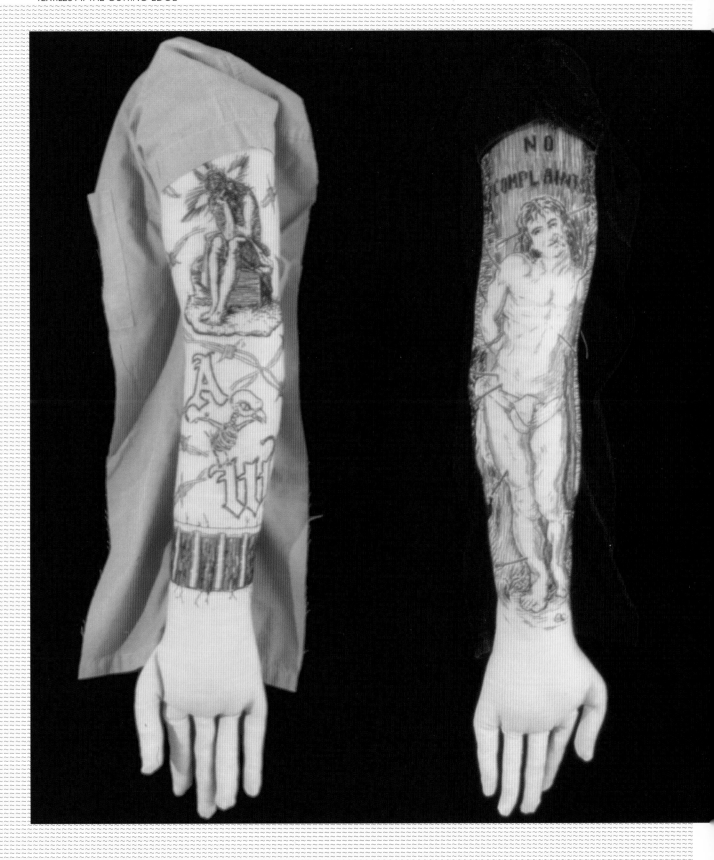

Benji Whalen, *Man of Sorrows*, 2005.
Embroidery floss on stuffed cotton, poly/cotton sleeve, 52 cm long.

Benji Whalen, *Jesus Christ (full arm portrait)*, 2007.
Embroidery floss on stuffed cotton, cotton sleeve, 54 cm long.

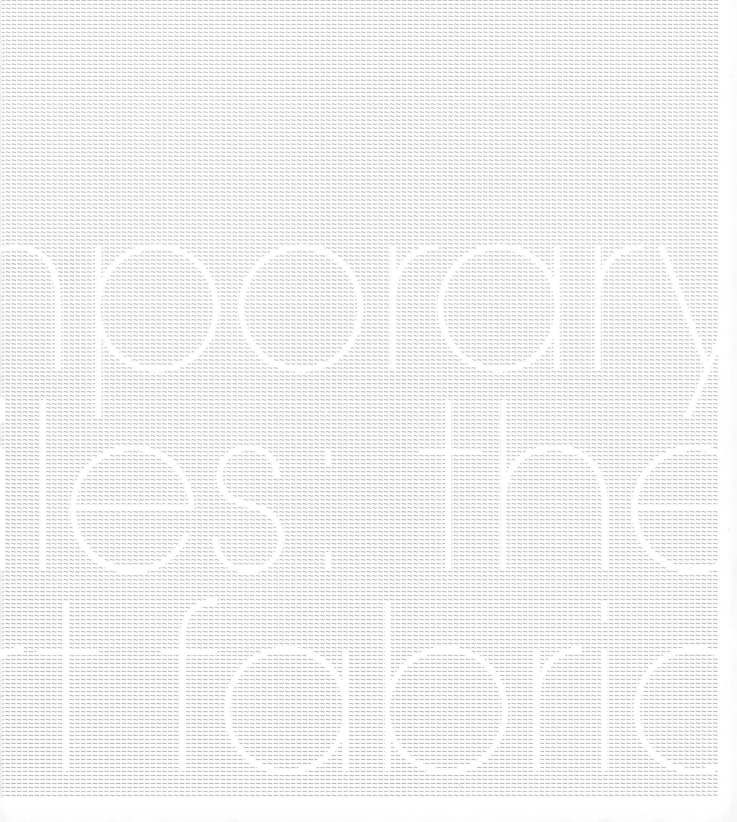

janis jefferies

histories, terms and definitions

In 1982, I wrote a paper, which was presented alongside the international exhibition, *Documenta*, in Kassel, Germany. It was written to coincide with an experimental show of work that related to a hybrid combination of what was called 'fine art' and textile practices, or 'soft art', which formed the foundation of *K-18* Kassel:

> The twentieth century has witnessed many experiments in the 'arts' initiated by new concepts and the use of new materials and techniques. Social, political and economic factors had radically altered the definitions of art and thus changed its meaning. Contiguous with these shifts, the nature, role and status of the decoration and the decorative arts need to be reconsidered. I asked the question, why 'art after Duchamp easily includes postcards but not tapestries, Xerox but not weaving'.[1]

This question was based on the exhibition and book that Mildred Constantine and Jack Lenor Larsen organised and published in 1980.[2] Entitled *The Art Fabric: Mainstream* both the exhibition and the book presented a range of textile (called fibre in America) placing an emphasis primarily on technique; their central chapter is titled "Expansion of Materials and Techniques", with subheadings such as "Paper", "Leather", "Felting and Fabric Embellishments" and "Dye Techniques". The research was based on their first collaboration, *Beyond Craft: The Art Fabric,* itself a 300 page volume representing a history of art fabric during the 1960s, which usefully provides several criteria for their usage of the term 'art fabric'.[3] The definition of the term includes everything from actual constructions (formed on or off the loom), parameters for understanding a work's relationship to tradition and notions of authorship. This was a benchmark moment in which the proliferation and use of a wide range of materials to create aesthetic parallels to painting and sculpture was pursued. Constantine and Larsen included many illustrations of work from wall hangings, environmentally-based installations and assemblages, noting that cloth—wrapped, compressed, or non-utilitarian—had played an early and important role within twentieth century art concepts. Beginning with Dadaist, Man Ray (who wrapped up a sewing machine), and continuing to Jeanne-Claude and Christo's clothed objects and wrapped Reichstag in Berlin, fabric was becoming highly visible within the visual arts. Even earlier in the "Technical Manifesto of Futurist Sculpture", Umberto Boccioni had incited us to: "Destroy the wholly literary and traditional nobility of marble and bronze.... Affirm that even 20 different materials can compete in a single work to effect plastic emotion! Let us enumerate some: glass, wood, cardboard, iron, cement, horsehair, leather, cloth, mirrors, electric lights, etc, etc."[4]

In fact, two generations later in a pioneering essay on Jackson Pollock, the 'happenings' performer, Allan Karpow declared in a similar manner to Boccioni, "Objects of every sort are materials for the new art: paint, chairs, food, electric and neon lights, smoke, water, old socks, a dog, movies, a thousand other things will be discovered by the present generation of artists."[5]

In one sense, both Boccioni and Kaprow were right and indeed many artists, the art world and its institutions, have dispensed with historical hierarchies of genres, materials and techniques. But, as forcibly argued by Constantine and Larsen, "the crafts, even when clearly outside the category of utility, are generally assigned a lower status that the 'fine' arts".[6] In these arguments textile is positioned within the category of craft and its many problematic histories and discourses.[7]

Nonetheless, what was, and remains, unique about *Beyond Craft: The Art Fabric* and *The Art Fabric: Mainstream* is that a number of marvellous installation shots, from exhibitions large and small originating in Lausanne, to the miniature textile biennials held at the British Crafts Centre in London from 1974–1980 are included in full colour with biographies on all the artists cited.[8] A number of installation shots were drawn from the international Lausanne Biennials, which characterised the increasing interest in the art fabrics, their structure and an analysis of their socio-historical importance.[9] Constantine and Larsen remain amongst a handful of art critics and writers to have explored the evolution of the art fabric and the prestige of the decorative arts in contemporary art practice.

Man Ray, *The Enigma of Isidore Ducasse, after the original of 1920*, 1971.
Sewing machine, wool & string. © Private Collection/ Peter Willi/ The Bridgeman Art Library.

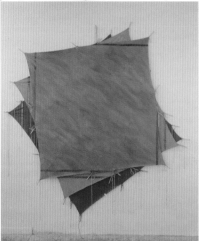

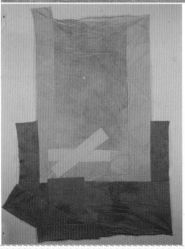

TOP TO BOTTOM

Magdalena Abakanowicz, *Black Garment*, 1969.
Sisal Weaving, 300 x 180 x 60 cm. Collection Stedelijk Museum, Amsterdam.
Photo: Artur Starewicz.

Richard Smith, *Three Square 2*, 1975.
Acrylic on canvas with aluminium rods and string–three canvases, 175 x 175 cm each.
British Council Collection. © The Artist and Flowers, London.

Stephenie Bergman, *T-TOTAL*, 1977.
Painted, dyed and washed cotton, sewn, 132 x 107 cm. © British Council Collection
and the artist.

In an influential attempt to address an audience beyond the art world, *The Art Fabric: Mainstream* begins with a historical framework identical to *Beyond Craft: The Art Fabric*, providing a summary of concepts introduced in the earlier volume, as well as initiating an interesting and important discussion on the large scope of works produced throughout the 1960s. Works by Sheila Hicks, Jagoda Buic and Magdalena Abakanowicz were influenced by the oversized canvases elemental to Abstract Expressionism, notably Jackson Pollock, Sam Gilliam and Lucas Samaras. As Jenni Sorkin asks, "was the art fabric at its height of recognition in the early years of the 1980s?".[10] Many of my contemporaries believe that it was. The 'art fabric' can be summarised as bringing into perspective the history of fabric in a larger sense. This was to include the characteristic flexibility and softness of textile works, the multiplicity of forms of a creative language that is unique to fibre and qualities of the decorative. Ideas around the decorative were certainly in vogue with a number of artists not represented in Constantine or Larsen's work, but their contribution did much to bring these methods and materials to the fore of critical discussion. I discuss the potential reasons for this and the artists that might have been included in what would have been a broader survey of contemporary practice through what became known as the Pattern and Decoration painters later on in this essay.

In my 1982 paper, "The Role of Soft Materials in Arts", I attempted to provide a (by no means exhaustive) survey of the development of certain tendencies that have occurred within painting, sculpture and the textile arts during the 1960s and 70s. However, I sought then (as now) to provide some observations on the relationship between the work being done in textiles and what was then described as 'fine' artists who used materials in their work as a primary means of expression. In this context, I discussed the work of two British artists, Stephanie Bergman and Richard Smith. In *T-Total*, 1977, Bergman cut, dyed and painted her washed pieces of canvas, drawing attention to the tactile qualities of their material.[11] For Bergman, the surface colour is achieved through staining diluted acrylic paint into the loose weave of the cloth. Smith produced a number of key works in the 1970s, for example *Threesquare 2*, 1975, and *Grey Path*, 1973, in which the stretcher was abandoned and the canvas transformed into kite-like, suspended forms. Both Bergman and Smith's work evidence a fascination with the canvas as textile, and the meanings inherent in that material nature.

The 'stain and soak' methods of the American painter Helen Frankenthaler and the 'all over' Colour Field paintings of Morris Louis were part of a whole range of 'skin-like' surfaces that were recognised as 'richly textile' in their associative qualities. Work by Eva Hesse (latex and cheesecloth), Michelle Stuart (paper and rope), Robert Morris (felt) and Barry Flanagan (dyed hessian cloths), all drew attention to both the nature and identity of the fabrics used and the structures that support them. Similarly, Robert Rauschenberg's *Bed*, 1955, used paint as well as cloth in the form of a found quilt, and Claes Oldenburg and Coosje van Bruggen's *Soft Bathtub (Model)—Ghost Version*, 1966, employs canvas stuffed with kapok, used to reproduce familiar household objects on an enormous scale. Christo and Jean-Claude's wrapped objects, soft packages and 5,600 cubic metre package for *Documenta 4*, Kassel, 1968, are other examples of this very 'fine art' preoccupation with textile as material. These soft sculptures were intended as sensual experiences and commentary on our material world, drawing the viewers' attention to haptic qualities. The emphasis on touch is physically intrinsic to art-making and our engagement with its surface materiality in close proximity.[12] All depiction in painting and sculpture implies haptic response to some degree, but the concept of touch is much expanded in the works cited above, through specific choices of tactile or ephemeral materials. In this context, fabric, cloth and that which makes textile, is useful both as a material term and as a conceptual strategy operating in the transformative power of metaphor, interweaving between words and things, surfaces and skins, fibre and material, touch and tactility. In fact, the literature on aesthetics and art history focuses largely on sight to the exclusion of all other senses (see, as just two of many possible examples, Hal Foster's *Vision and Visuality* and Jonathan Crary's *Techniques of the Observer: On Vision and Modernity in the Nineteenth Century*). This is, in itself, an instance of a larger phenomenon, as sight has historically been the most privileged of all the senses. That is to say, the role of touch in the production, appreciation and handling of artefacts from a wide cultural base has been neglected, perhaps in part due to the philosophy that the senses cannot be the medium of an elevated aesthetic experience. In a visual culture such as the west, touch has only recently re-emerged to take a place at the forefront of the senses.

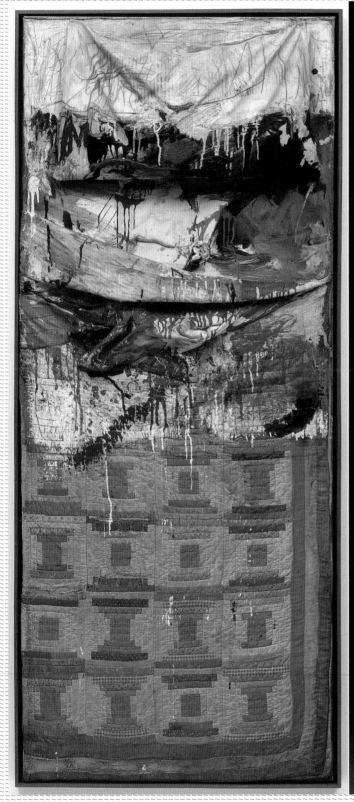

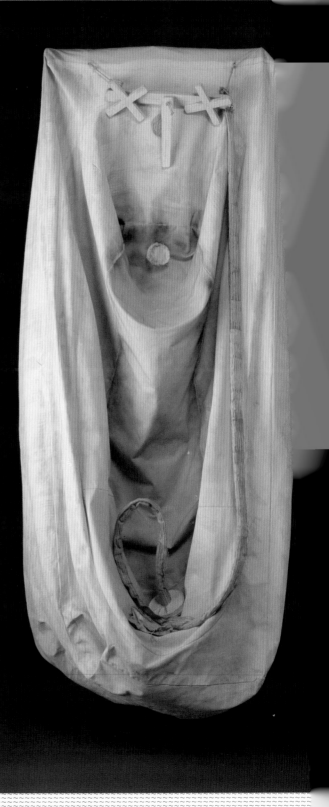

Robert Raushenberg, *Bed*, 1955.
Combine painting: oil and pencil on pillow, quilt, and sheet on wood supports, 191.1 x 80 x 20.3 cm. Gift of Leo Castelli in honor of Alfred H Barr. © 2008. Digital image, courtesy of The Museum of Modern Art, New York/Scala, Florence.

Claes Oldenburg, *Soft Bathtub (Model)—Ghost Version*, 1966.
Acrylic and pencil on foam-filled canvas with wood cord and plaster, 204.7 x 89.8 x 89.8 cm. Hirshhorn Museum and Sculpture Garden, Smithsonian Institution, Joseph H Hirshhorn Purchase Fund, 1998. Photo: Lee Stalsworth.

Michelle Stuart, *Hard Garden History*, 1975.
Rock pounded muslin on rag paper, earth from Hyde Park, twine, 33 x 25.4 x 3.17 cm.

Morris Louis, *Gamma Epsilon*, 1960.
Private Collection © The Bridgeman Art Library.

Peter and Ritzi Jacobi, *Romanica*, 1978.
330 x 950 x 100 cm. Photo: Dirk Bakker, the Arts Institute Detroit, 1981.

In Britain, and surely influenced by what was happening in America, Michael Brennand-Wood believed that the impact of Bergman, Smith, Hesse, Rauschenberg, and the *Decor Show* seen at the Museum of Modern Art in Oxford during 1980, genuinely challenged the role and place that fibre and material, touch and tactility had within the historical hierarchies and restrictions of genre. This, he argued, was due to the additional emphasis placed on the tactile qualities of textile when combined with non-utilitarian concepts. The terms of reference within which contemporary textiles are produced have altered. The effect of this change is not fully realised, but there is evidence in certain current work of a change in awareness and the past constraints of use, durability and application which have begun to break down. Textiles will never again be a definable area; in the same way, distinctions between painting and sculpture have become pointless.[13]

Revisiting the debate some 30 years later, it is evident that there is once again a cultural re-evaluation of textiles with a number of artists who define themselves as painters, but refer both to textiles and painting in their work, either directly through the quotation of historical references to pattern, or through reference to the materiality and tactile qualities of fabrics deployed in their method. Both tendencies 'comfortably' reference the elasticity of the term 'decorative', promoting a significant aesthetic strategy within contemporary art practices that produce hybrid forms that fit into no one genre exclusively. This is something that I take up in "What's in a Name?" at the end of this essay. Currently, a renewed interest in surface and structure, decoration and detail, material and process recalls the Supports/Surfaces Movement in France during the 1970s. This represents a shift in attitude towards decoration (and particularly pattern) within an inclusive definition of visual arts. The 1990s witnessed a resurgence of an expanded recognition of decorative applications in art. This resurgence can be seen in the many contemporary art works that use a variety of textile-based, material methods of making, as well as in textile studio practices that move beyond material and technique as historically outlined in *Beyond Craft: The Art Fabric* and *The Art Fabric: Mainstream*.

pattern and decoration: america

Until the 1960s, there had been a general agreement within visual arts practice that fine art consisted of two categories, painting and sculpture. As a young woman and painting student studying at art college in the early 1970s, I can testify to this statement though I was also part of a generation that challenged these categories in order to break down the rigidity of the old system of craft/art hierarchies. Whilst some of my contemporaries ventured into 'happenings' and performance, I went 'off-canvas' to 'off-loom' constructions and continued to work with materials and form. I discovered that shapes could be more structural when formed through the off-loom process of weaving. In was a moment of entering the 'other,' a textile domain and its uneasy relation to the middle ground that my work occupied between art and craft. The sex of the artist mattered, it was a time of intense reading, argument and re-writing the canons of art history. Rosizka Parker and Griselda Pollock's book, *Old Mistresses: Women, Art and Ideology* was one key texts of the time.[14] Their writing traces the ideas and value systems about art, artists, femininity and creativity to demonstrate the position that women have occupied within culture and art history. It is worth reprinting one of the seminal concepts from a text that outlined the book's genesis in the art history collective to which Parker and Pollock belonged, first printed in the journal *Spare Rib* in 1981:

> This division in the so-called 'fine art' extends to the distinction between art and craft. Women's practice in the forms of art using needle and thread have been dismissed as painstaking and merely dexterous, while great art is defined as intellectually testing and truly inventive, qualities that are only exercised by men. These differences have been misrepresented to us as hierarchical division between great art and lesser decorative crafts. Art history represents this division to us as self-evident and natural whereas what women make is accorded a lesser value and regard.[15]

Now viewed as a classic feminist text, *Women, Art and Ideology* paved the way for a re-thinking of themes repressed in Modernist aesthetics. The decorative, craft and the domestic became challenging ideas that women in the fine arts could engage through work involving textiles. Though their achievements in this sphere are often highly thought of, the fact that painters like Nathalie Goncharova, Alexandra Exter, Liubov Popova, Annie Albers, Sophia Taeuber-Arp, Vanessa Bell and Sonia Delaunay were involved in textile design, weaving, tapestry and costume-making, has equivocal implications. On the one hand, for a woman artist to 'return' as it were, to a prescribed traditional role in the minor arts (the decorative, craft and the domestic) generally less conducive to fame and financial gain than a career in painting or sculpture, can be seen as a step backwards from a feminist point of view. It therefore becomes highly problematic, even contradictory, for women artists to acknowledge textile practices within their work without recognising the underlying hierarchical value system and hierarchical divisions outlined by Parker and Pollock. The interventions of these Modernist pioneers into mainstream art history gave confidence to many women of my generation. Textile and the decorative offered the possibility to rethink their contribution as part of a broader women's movement while still remaining within the mainstream of visual arts practices.

Many young women studying painting in art school in the early 1970s became disillusioned with the dominance of masculine and Eurocentric tendencies in art. The critical rhetoric of Clement Greenberg and his formalist purism symbolised closure for many young practitioners and forms a telling structure for discussions of changing values at the time. For Greenberg, self-referential autonomy, a fixed point of origin of identity, assumed it was possible to draw boundaries around the aesthetic 'frame'. The critic's role within this model was to pay attention to the specifics of the practice in question. Greenberg's view was based on a moral judgement, that is, 'purity in art' was a means of preserving a living western culture. However, for Jonathon Harris, Greenberg established a kind of closed judgement about values of good and bad art, and what constituted 'authentic' art practice.[16] In his now famous essay, "Avant Garde and Kitsch", Greenberg holds mass culture responsible for creating a new kind of kitsch and 'low' culture, and fills the gap between the latter and Avant-Garde Art with a wealth of anti-decorative rhetoric.[17] Christopher Reed quotes from another of Greenberg's important theoretical texts, *The Crisis of Easel Painting,* 1948. Here Greenberg writes:"The 'fatal' influence of 'all-over' abstract art, which, because 'it comes very close to decoration—to the kind seen in wallpaper patterns that can be repeated indefinitely, now 'infects' painting as a whole."[18]

The words "repeated indefinitely" and "infects" are significant here. Christopher Reed elaborates: for Greenberg, the only value of decoration was to destroy itself by becoming "vehement", "turbid", and "violent". Part of the "mission" of Modernist painting, Greenberg said, was "to find ways of using the decorative against itself".[19] Greenberg's propensity to invoke the decorative in order to deny it recalls Loos' polemics against the "criminal" decorative. Greenberg's derogatory reference to wallpaper and its unlimited propensity for ornamental repetition are highly significant, because it evokes domestic space as representative of the reviled decorative as a whole. Wallpaper was nothing more than decoration in its most superficial form and worth invoking only in anticipation of its own self-destruction. By connecting the decorative to mass culture, wallpaper, and kitsch, Greenberg affirmed a blanket discrimination against these categories. Modern Art was much more than home decoration, and the risk of it being viewed as wallpaper potentially undermined the high ambitions of the Modernist project. Greenberg often aligned painters who failed to conform to his criteria of absolute, pictorially flat abstraction with the decorative or interior domestic space. For Greenberg, the domestic is the antithesis of art and decoration is devoid of the essential properties that constitute authentic art. Preservation and purity were qualities that stood against any extra-pictorial pollution. It finds existence within itself. Self-referential autonomy is often described as "art for art's sake". As painting and sculpture were wholly entrenched in their mediums, to be isolated and defined, so it became one fear amongst many (of its own otherness) that decoration became the spectra that haunts modern painting.[20] The Greenbergian form of Modernism tended to be gendered and medium-specific. He marginalised a large number of diverse practices that arose, notably, in the work of Robert Rauschenberg whose production of installation and assemblage works were rejected because of their affiliation with vernacular culture. This blind spot in Greenberg's and other Modernist critical writers' work, created a potential resource which continues to be deployed in cultural critical thought this day.

Detail, the minute and intricate attention to pattern, is acknowledged as having the potential to destabilise an internal ordering of surface structure. Detail participates in a larger semantic field, bonded on the one hand by the ornamental by its connotation of effeminacy and decadence, and on the other by the everyday, whose prissiness is rooted in the domestic sphere presided over by women.[21] At the beginning of the twentieth century, Adolf Loos accused ornament, and by implication decoration, of the crime of turning back the clock of cultural development. In the essay "Ornament and Crime", 1908, Loos argues that all ornament can be traced

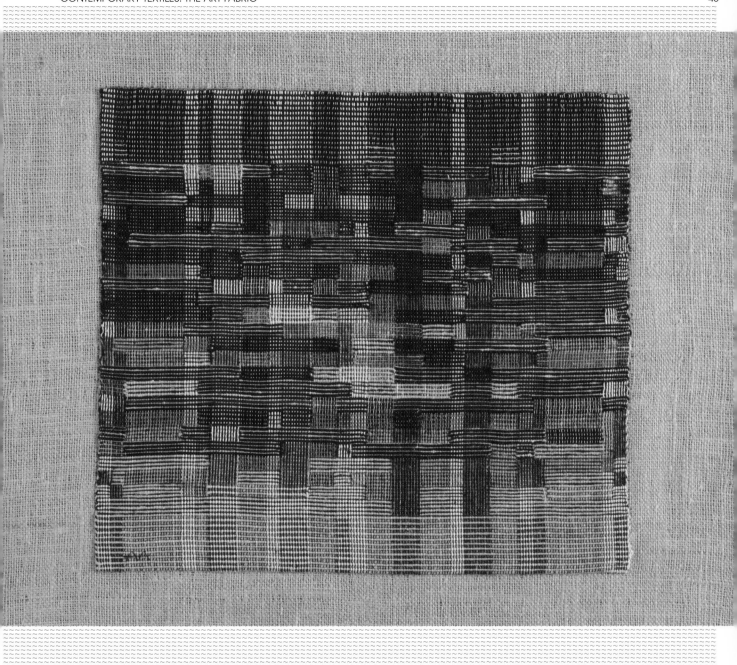

Anni Albers, *Tapestry*, 1948.
Hand-woven linen and cotton, 41.9 x 47.6 cm. Edgar Kaufmann Jr Purchase Fund.
Digital image © The Museum of Modern Art/Licensed by SCALA/ Art Resource, NY.

Joyce Kozloff, *Three Facades*, 1973.

Robert Zakanitch, *Elephant Rose*, 1978.

Jo Bruton *Ken-tucky*, 2002.
From the exhibition *Walk Slowly Towards the Light* at Matt's Gallery from 17 April–9 June 2002. Image courtesy of the artist and Matt's Gallery, London.

to childish graffiti—sexual images smeared with faecal matter.[22] He saw the same impulse manifested in the practice of tattooing, claiming that only savages and criminals bear tattoos. Decoration represents only the lowest of human impulses for Loos, and so it must be stripped from art and design, especially from useful objects.

The taste for the decorative was pathologised as feminine, as embellishment, as style, as frivolous, as excessive and was therefore constantly repressed within the rhetorical devices of Modernism. Detail and fabric were viewed as decorative extras and excluded from the rigid confines of the regularly ordered space in the pictorial plane. Once released, detail and pattern become excessively magnified and erupt, even exceeded the borders which once tried to contain them. In his discussion of ornament Mick Carter observes that, with all its association in adornment and decoration, ornament has a tendency to wander from its proper place, threatening and undermining the aesthetic value of an artwork. Drawing on Derrida's suspicions of any rigid distinction between essential and non-essential (supplementary) registers, Carter argues that it is only within the play, the tensions between ornamental errancy and the confines of the picture frame, is meaning created.[23] This argument becomes all the more powerful when viewing works produced within what has become known as the Pattern and Decoration Movement of the 1970s. There were several artists who played with the decorative as ornamental errancy, utilising mobile space in which new forms of practice could emerge. Kim MacConnel—along with artists such as Tina Girouard, Valerie Jaudon, Jane Kaufman, Joyce Kozloff, Robert Kushner, Miriam Schapiro and Robert Zakanitch—each expressed a wide range of influences in their work, from ethnographic textiles, hooked rug kits, linoleum kitchen tiles, ancient Islamic enameling, stenciled wallpaper, Indian saris, colonial quilts, Persian kilims, Henri Matisse's cut-outs and American craft traditions.

I have suggested that an emphasis on pattern and decoration in the twenty-first century is in part derived from feminism and feminist ideas of re-thinking an old system of artistic hierarchy, expressing a critique of the blanket discrimination against these categories. There is once again a renewed interest in fabric, cloth and textile and a sense that the inviolate distinction between the 'fine arts' and 'decorative arts' was, and continues to be, artificial. Indeed, as I have argued elsewhere, there was an unprecedented amount of material fabrication and stitch manipulation going on during the 1990s in Britain and the America.[24] Artists began to incorporate techniques generally associated with the domestic realm and female-associated textile-like processes. This form of making as an aesthetic, conceptual strategy has become a significantly effective means to bridge the gap between high and low, fine and applied art, home and the world, gender and identity. Whether it is Gary Hume's love of tapestry's flora and fauna details, or Chris Ofili's lashings of deliciously coloured and unashamedly sensual paint; Jo Bruton's hand-made collages of pattern painting and glass beads surfaces, or the use of highly patterned soft fabrics that make up Laura Ford's work, many contemporary British artists flirt with decorative possibilities in practices which were once taboo within art institutions and academies. As I have written elsewhere, this strategy, in my view, hotly contests any notion of an 'anti-handmadeness', particularly in British art. Motifs from textiles, architecture and ceramics are appropriated and applied to painting mimicking and disturbing Greenbergian formalism and the prescriptions of the Modernist aesthetics typical of the twentieth century.

The Pattern and Decoration Movement unleashed the possibilities for the co-existence of fine art and craft, on the same canvas, incorporating a 1970s trend toward the inclusion of decorative motifs and the often undervalued, excluded material they inhabit—lace, fabric, wallpaper, carpets and pattern—into the production and discourses of art. The sensual aspects of art could be played with, enjoyed and be part of cultural critique that suited many women who wanted to explore 'women's work' as part of a more personal means of expression.

The artist Miriam Schapiro was a key and influential figure during the 1970s. I became aware of Schapiro through the American journals, *Artforum* and *Art in America*, both of which were held in my art school library. Later on, I was able to access Schapiro's own writings through the American feminist journal, *Heresies*.[27] Schapiro started experimenting with pattern, decoration, and craft-based materials and practices during her involvement with the feminist art programme at CalArts in Valencia, the *Womanhouse* project (with Judy Chicago) in Los Angeles, and her teaching at the University of California, San Diego. Schapiro embellished her work with many decorative qualities referencing domestic and textile processes like patchwork and quilting. Patterned cloth became the material

Laura Ford, *Glory Glory 1*, 2005.
Steel plaster and mixed media, Shown at the Venice Biennale, 2005. Image courtesy the artist and Houldsworth, London.

Judy Chicago with Myriam Schapiro: catalog cover for *Womanhouse*, 1972.
designed by Sheila de Bretteville. Image courtesy of Through the Flower Archives.

Valerie Jaudon, *Jackson*, 1976.
Metallic pigment in polymer emulsion and pencil on canvas, 183.0 x 183.0 cm. Gift of
Joseph H Hirshhorn, 1977.

on which she worked partly to legitimise her experience as an artist and to validate the traditional activities of women. The fan, once a quaint female accessory, became a three and a half metre geometric blaze of colour and pattern. Her series, *Femmages*, includes kimonos, fans, hearts and various other explorations of domesticity. Many *Femmages* were complex decorative collages produced on a large scale. The American critic and writer Linda Nochlin noted in 1973 that Schapiro's work was, "impassioned yet controlled sensuous extremism", "daring out of the reductive corner which much mainstream abstraction has painted itself".[28]

Schapiro was one of a group of artists who first met in New York in 1975. Together with those cited previously, and the influential art critic Amy Goldin, they loosely formed what became to be known as the Pattern Painters.[29] According to Carrie Rickey, their ideas about pattern ran in parallel to painter and neologist Mario Yrisarry, who is credited with the term Pattern Painting. At the time, Goldin was analysing the potential of the ornamental register for architecture, and became pivotal in drawing together artists whose work focused on the decorative. Pattern, as Goldin lucidly explained, is not determined by the repetition of a motif, instead she wrote that pattern is created by the constancy of the intervals between motifs. Artists and critics met in a studio that Goldin established in Soho, which quickly turned into an alternative exhibition space in West Broadway. Inspired by the abundance of fabrics in downtown commercial and ethnic neighbourhoods, the 'group' organised *Ten Approaches to the Decorative* in 1976 at Allesandra Gallery. Holly Solomon, a particularly supportive gallerist, put on a number of Pattern and Decoration shows promoting Kushner, MacConnel and Jaudon's work. One of the writers for *Artforum* at the time, John Perrault, described this painting style as "non-minimalist, non-sexist, historically conscious, sensuous, romantic, rational, decorative".[31] Like patterning itself, Pattern Painting was viewed as "two-dimensional, non-hierarchical, all over, a-centric, and anionic".[32] Perrault recognised the Movement as a challenge to the divisions between fine and decorative arts, referring to weaving and mosaics as essential qualities to the patterning elements. He was quite explicit in his claim that the grid was the basis of all patterning and that weaving was its true source by virtue of the way in which the lines of the "warp and weft make up the primordial square block grid".[33] In 1977, Perrault organised *Pattern Painting* at PS 1, New York to showcase the work coming out of the Movement at the time. Writing in the *Village Voice*, April Kingsley suggested that Perreault's tenacity combined with the alternative spirit of PS 1 had made for an exhibition that centred on the core Movement consisting of work by nearly two-thirds women artists and one-third unknown artists, in an attempt to avoid market and institutional pressure to legitimise the group with more established practitioners.[34] Another key advocate and writer at the time was Jeff Perone. Perone, Perrault, Rickey and Goldin provided the exposure and critical framing in the art press necessary to raise the profile of the Pattern Painting Movement. Perone was particularly forceful in his praise for those exhibiting in *Ten Approaches to the Decorative*.[35] In his review of the show, Perone emphasised:

> It is, in fact another irony that decoration is accused of being emotionally sterile. For the painter of the last 20 years has been convinced that a physical flatness should be equated with an emotional flatness. On the other hand, work, which is called 'decorative', can cease to be only about itself and begin to explore other kinds of experience. It wants to accumulate details, image and space (collage) and discuss a variety of references. Narrow references to art history are replaced with various cultural signs and designs of general and multivalent meaning.[36]

Perone observed that other, more inclusive surveys addressing the "decorative impulse" were perhaps beneficial for revealing the trend to be "a wide-ranging phenomenon" that was "open" rather than "closed", but such efforts also risked diluting Pattern and Decoration and its specific implications.[37]

The Pattern and Decoration artists reintroduced textile, patterned fabric and decorative practices such as collage, embroidery, sewing and weaving into their paintings. These artists also privileged ornament for its hedonistic sensuousness, eccentricity and playfulness. The decorative became an empowering tool for the members of this group in their desire for an inclusive approach to art that would incorporate past and potential decorative iconography from diverse contexts into mainstream artistic practice. Jourdan drew on pattern blocks to provide her with vast sources of decoration from around the world and in this sense, prefigured the archival research of The Pattern Lab discussed later in this essay. These artists all engaged the history of the decorative in particular ways, Kozloff worked from designs and patterns from American Indian blankets and rugs, Kusher hand-painted his fabrics and MacConnel joined patterned strips of material and found fabrics to form larger canvases of hanging fabric that never quite matched up.

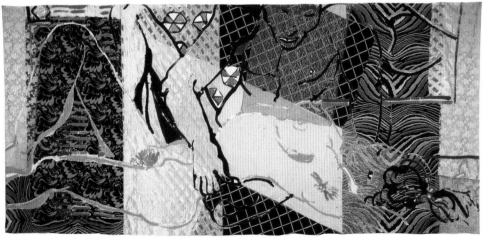

†Miriam Schapiro. *Anatomy of a Kimono,* detail, 1975–1976.
Fabric and acrylic on canvas, ten panels, total length 15.8 m. Image courtesy of Galerie
Bruno Bischofberger, Zurich, Switzerland. Photo: Greg Staley. From the exhibition *Claiming
Space: Some American Feminist Originators,* American University Museum.

Robert Kushner, *Tryst,* 1983.
Acrylic on cotton with mixed fabric, 259.1 x 532 cm. Private Collection, NY. Photo
courtesy DC Moore Gallery, NY.

Yinka Shonibare, *Scramble for Africa*, 2003.
14 figures, 14 chairs, table, 132 x 488 x 280 cm. Commissioned by the Museum for
African Art, New York, for the exhibition *Looking Both Ways*. Image courtesy the artist and
Stephen Friedman Gallery, London.

Together, Jourdan and Kozloff compiled quotations from art historians revealing the sexist basis of historical judgements on the use of textile and the decorative in fine art. Called *Art Hysterical Notions of Progress and Culture,* they sought to expose assumptions of art history, and the marginal positioning of the decorative in order to pinpoint the importance of language in shaping the concepts of art history as a discipline. Around the same time, a special issue of *Heresies* was dedicated to "Women's Traditional Arts: The Politics of Aesthetics".[38]

One of Kozloff's major concerns was western dominance over non-western visual idioms. She drew on pre-Columbian artefacts and Islamic ornamental traditions, and borrowed eclectically from these practices, reinterpreting their iconography through various media, including printed textiles, to produce 'hommages' that foregrounded her concerns. This approach also became the basis for a series of paintings she completed after visiting Morocco and Turkey in the mid to late 1970s. She transformed the patterns from these cultures into large paintings that bridged a western aesthetic language and the non-western sources she quoted in the work. Kozloff transformed the patterns from pre-Columbian places of worship and her travels to Morocco and Turkey into large paintings, which became a personal compilation of decorative miscellany that merged different textile techniques of fabric printing and mosaic work into large decorative presentations that covered the gallery walls and floor. Her excessive use of the decorative can be compared to Yinka Shonibare's painted, patterned textile work in the sense that Jourdan's strategy was also intended to communicate a socio-political message through the medium of textile as material and as sign. It is the deliberate use of pattern as a conveyer of a meaning related to inter-cultural relationships that connect the two artists. Where Kozloff borrows and transforms patterns from many parts of the world, Shonibare paints on and plays with the identity of patterned textiles to create visual chaos. This ambition is evident in his paintings from the 1990s like *Double Dutch*, 1994 and *Feather Pink*, 1997. These works are usually installations of small squares, painted panels of 'African' fabric. The history of fabric used, the ambiguous materials and motifs of west African textiles, seem to symbolise the rich complexity of postcolonial cultures in that, while the patterns and colours are thought to be authentically African, they actually originate from Indonesian Batik work, a technique which was industrialised by Dutch traders historically active in Africa. Shonibare underlines the visual pleasure of the amoebic textile patterns, as the work becomes a metaphor for excess and exploitation. His symbolic use of textiles is perhaps most clear in the work *Maxa*, a vast wall painted blue and covered in different sized and patterned discs.[39]

> The fabric carries with it a kind of fallacy, if you like. I started using the fabrics to make paintings but to do the opposite of a large heroic painting, to fragment them to smaller pieces, which then negates this notion of the grand, big, white, male, heroic object. Of course the feminist movement challenged this kind of patriarchal way of presenting art and so a lot of the art that developed.[40]

Shonibare readily acknowledges he is "definitely challenging Greenberg's Modernist notions of purity, polluting". He sees his use of fabric as drawing 'low culture' and 'tacky crafts' into the so-called 'high art' space.

Linked in the 1970s to the Pattern and Decoration Movement, Valerie Jaudon's restrained translations of decorative motifs combined visual quotations from non-western decorative traditions. In her essay for the catalogue of the 1996 Jaudon retrospective, art historian Anna C Chave fully explores the Pattern and Decoration Movement as context for Jaudon's early work, rightly emphasising the distinctly feminist inflection of the Movement.[41] As Chave observes, quoting the art historian EH Gombrich, decorative richness offers "a feast for the eye without demanding that we should taste every dish".[42] Interestingly, Gombrich analysed two functions of perception in respect of decorative richness and pattern. For him, these were associated with the differences between the presentation of form in pictorial and pattern art—looking at order and scanning for order, with the cognitive skills associated with these two functions drawn along gender lines.[44] Pattern Art has been historically noted as a sign for repetitiousness of women's work and was explained away as a reflection of the repetitious nature of women's domestic duties. It is these ideas that were challenged by Parker and Pollock in their *Pattern Painting* show in 1977, which consisted of work by nearly two-thirds women artists, as previously noted.

The Pattern and Decoration Movement was a relatively brief one, but no less significant. Its importance lies partly in the revival of interest in textiles (indeed a number of craft-based practices) and a sense that the inviolate distinction between

LEFT TO RIGHT

Jim Isermann, *Untitled (Fabric Wall Hanging)*, 1993.
Cotton and cotton blend, approximately 182.9 x 182.9 cm. Image courtesy of the artist
and Richard Telles Fine Art.

Jim Hodges, *You*, 1997.
Silk flowers and thread, 548.64 x 487.68 cm. In collaboration with the Fabric Workshop
and Museum, Philadelphia, Collection of the Fabric Workshop and Museum,
Philadelphia.

the 'fine arts' and 'decorative arts' was always artificial. There were various attempts to legitimate the Movement, but as Admason suggests there was not a theoretical apparatus to underpin its sustained visibility, though recent exhibitions have tried to reassess and appraise the Movement's historical significance.[45] For example, in 2003, curator and art critic Michael Duncan curated two large group shows: *NYPD: New York Pattern & Decoration*, at Shoshana Wayne Gallery and *LAPD: Los Angeles Pattern & Decoration* at Rosamund Felsen Gallery. Comprising 35 works by 16 artists, *NYPD* focused primarily on key Pattern and Decoration practitioners; Schapiro's *Curtains*, 1972, express her fascinating lace work, whilst Jaudon, Kozloff, Kushner and MacConnel evidenced the group's enthusiasm for lines and motifs from non-western and ethnic architecture, decor, fabric and clothing, and Zakanitch's grid-based floral pattern painting revealed the Movement's propensity to play off and elaborate upon the codes and underpinnings of high Modernism. However brief their prominence, the impact of the Pattern and Decoration practitioners on a generation of younger American artists like Polly Afpelbaum (floor sheets of red, crushed velvet, dyed fabrics) Jim Isermann (tartan wall weaves, rugs and fabric wall hangings), and Jim Hodges is evident.[46] Hodge's, *Every Touch*, 1995, acknowledges the thousands of gestures involved in disassembling artificial flowers and reassembling them into a five by four metre curtain.[47] In trying to create the effect of lace, Hodges cut multicoloured fabric petals from hundreds of plastic stems, and arranged the pieces in 61 by 91 centimetre sections, pinning each petal to a large sheet of paper towel. Hodge's exploration of decoration, appropriation, women's issues and ideas around the domestic is often compared to Simon Periton; a British artist whose paper cut-out sculptures also recalls lace textile.

supports/surfaces: france

The broadly materialist preoccupation of Supports/Surfaces in many ways prefigures the reappraisal of the tropes of abstraction that was happening in New York. If American Colour Field painting in the early 1960s influenced Supports/Surfaces, it is equally likely that in turn the French group had an effect on the American Pattern and Decoration artists in the 1970s. There are striking parallels between the two Movements both in terms of the use of cloth, fabric, textile and decoration. Use of floor and wall, folding, printing, weaving and dying were consistent working strategies for Supports/Surfaces. For Simon Hantai, it meant a new folding technique of canvas, by working with the material folded on the ground, covering it with paint and then unfolding it again. For Francois Rouan it meant canvases were painted two at a time, cut into strips, woven again, marked with other criss crossings forming diagonal lines of squares unifying the two related surfaces.[48] His 'tressages' or woven paintings appear as an enlargement of the original canvas' warp and weft.

Supports/Surfaces were a loosely formed group of French artists, formally existing between 1967 and 1974, and included Daniel Buren, Olivier Mosset, Michel Parmentier, and Niele Toroni, Andre-Pierre Aarnal, Vincent Bioules, Daniel Buren, BMPT Group, Louis Cane, Marc Devade, Daniel Dezeuze, Noel Dolla, Toni Grand, Bernard Pages, Jean-Pierre Pincemin, Patrick Saytour, Andre Valensi and Claude Viallat. The feeling that painting had still not come to terms with its most basic conventions informed the group's name, which also proclaimed the materialist basis to the project of the Supports/Surfaces artists. These artists held that despite Greenberg's views, most painters (and they were mostly painters) showed little concern with the essential conditions of their medium. Their strategy was to show what was hidden, to deconstruct and individualise each of painting's elements. That is to say, they sought to isolate the two principal constituent elements of conventional painting (canvas and stretcher), to strip the medium down to its very material foundations. The first exhibition of the Supports/Surfaces group opened in 1970 at the Museum of Modern Art in Paris. Dezeuze and Viallat took charge of both the organisation of the exhibition and the critical texts that supported the ideas that formed the basis for the group in a larger sense.

The 'Surfaces', or canvas group, included Viallat, Cane, Pincemin, Saytour, Valensi, Dolla and Arnal, all of whom, in one way or another, worked with unstretched canvas. Viallat used a kind of stencil technique in which a single form is repeated in regular intervals on unstretched canvas. He employed tinting, staining and imprinting and any method of getting colour onto the canvas as long as it didn't require the traditional brush. The group stained, imprinted, bleached, faded, folded, dyed, crumpled and burned their works' surfaces, placing the canvases

Claude Viallat, *UNTITLED NO 52*, 2001.
Acrylic on beach umbrella, 217 x 163 cm. Image courtesy of the artist and Cheim & Read, New York.

on the floor or stacked as ladders to allow the viewer multiple entry points to the work. While Viallat favoured a strongly decorative art, like all the members of Supports/Surfaces he also sought to question prevailing assumptions about painting. Quite early, in 1966, he showed a canvas that he had signed every ten centimetres, thus allowing it to be cut and sold in fragments, like fabric. His canvases could float or be folded, rolled, raised on the ground, hooked directly to the wall or ceiling as assembled sewed painted surfaces.

Supports/Surfaces, as a movement, was drawn to thinness, softness and flexibility, often utilising traditionally domestic techniques like weaving and tinting, and effectively distancing themselves from the myth of 'heroic' painting, Greenbergian aesthetics and fixed structural forms. The Jeu de Paume's exhibition of Supports/Surfaces in 1998 was an attempt to reappraise its significance just as the aforementioned two large group shows: *NYPD: New York Pattern & Decoration* and *LAPD: Los Angeles Pattern & Decoration,* attempted to accomplish for the Pattern Painters.[49]

pattern and decoration: britain

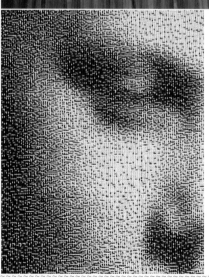

During the summer of 2002, you could also go to see *Pattern Crazy*.[50] Co-curated by British ceramicist Carol McNicoll and Jacqui Poncelet, ceramicist turned Pattern Painter, their combined passion for pattern took centre stage at the Crafts Council's gallery in Islington, London. Each pattern in the Gallery told a story, some more arresting than others. Bashir Makhoul's bullet-holed wallpaper referenced the bullet holes scarring the walls of Beirut whilst Brian Eno attempted to mesmerise the viewer with his computer-generated visual works. *Pattern Crazy* embraced the use of pattern in its widest sense, from Ian Grant's use of marquetry in his tartan top tables, to Julie Westbury's constructed collages of religious iconography made from an array of colourful postcards from the 1950s. Louise Taylor, at the time the director of exhibitions at the Crafts Council, never had her doubts. "Pattern is back in vogue", she affirms, "and this exhibition is taking a timely look at the subject". The reason it has taken such an age to wean the stylish set off of all things neutral and plain, according to Poncelet, is a knee-jerk prejudice against pattern.[51] Poncelet's obsession with this practice can be seen in *Carpet,* 1992, an asymmetrical cubist extravaganza first shown at London's South Bank centre, and in her fabric-based Pattern Paintings that formed part of her solo show called *The Decorative Sublime* held at the Museum of Modern Art in Oxford during 1994. The press release for this show immediately locates her work within a well-documented area of feminist concern when it states: "Like a number of artists of her generation she has refused to observe the boundaries between what has conventionally been regarded as craft and fine art." The exhibition consisted of two bodies of work, paintings on fabric or composite paintings and carpet pieces placed on the floor. These 'composite paintings' consisted of many small adjoining panels, some of which were reshown in a collaborative exhibition with Laura Ford at London's Camden Arts Centre during 1999. Called, *a Stranger Here Myself,* it was one of a series of three exhibitions organised by the Centre in 1999 and 2000 that explored the boundaries between the concepts of 'art' and 'craft'.[52] Simon Periton's successful incorporation of the decorative can be attributed to his singular approach to technique, refined over many years, and acknowledging the labour intensive processes that reference the practices of lace and textiles. As is often the case with ornament, both precision and repetition are important criteria. *Breathless,* 1998, seductive in its laciness, is a paper cut-out of a pair of blue lungs which forms part of a series of work on lung cancer exhibited at Periton's Camden Arts Centre exhibition. His use of non-repetitive pattern making at times echoes the disruptive intentions of Matisse's paper-cut work.

In pattern-based practice, repeated forms are presented in merged space. Meaning is consequently derived from the viewer attending to the repeated intervals and arrangements of patterned elements, viewed simultaneously. An overall arrangement is scanned in a never-ending process of engagement within the changeable worlds of appearance, perception and meaning. Robin Leher describes this kind of scanning from the artist's point of view:

> In this context, I am using pattern as a verb rather than as a noun. It is a way of seeing the world, a process by which to take in and make coherent the random and often chaotic information the world has to offer. It is the thread of my connections, which makes the world intelligible to me. The act of connecting... of 'patterning' provides a structure through which is sieved new information.[53]

TOP TO BOTTOM

Jacqui Poncelet, *Carpet,* 1994.
Arts Council Collection. Photo: Susanna Heron.

Lia Cook, *Face Maps, Halfseen,* 2005.
Textile, woven cotton, 26.7 cm x 20.3 cm. © Lia Cook. Collection of the Cooper-Hewitt Museum, Smithsonian, NY.

Lia Cook's *New Master Draperies* series provides this kind of scanning by representing cloth (as a sign of interior drapery) as both subject matter and the material object of her textile practice.[54] Her painted, dyed, and woven cloths magnify and repattern the expunged details of the Old Masters, liberating the pattern to simultaneously *realise* cloth and *represent* cloth.[55]

the pattern lab

Kathleen Mullaniff, Jennifer Wright and Jane Langley have been curating exhibitions that relate to textiles since the year 2000. They have been able to support artists who want to explore and interpret both historical and contemporary textile collections and archives. In 2001, *Spin* was researched and organised at the Victoria and Albert Museum and *Space Craft* researched at the Constance Howard Resource and Research Centre in Textiles at Goldsmiths University. In 2004, *Purl* was developed in response to the wallpaper and textile collections held at the Museum of Domestic Design and Architecture at Middlesex University and *Fabric: Interpreting the House* was developed in response to the Abbot Hall and Art Gallery's 40 year anniversary.[56] In 2003, *Loop* took place at the Bankfield Museum in Halifax (Britain), in which ideas around pattern, decoration and ornament once again predominated. Indeed, such ideas have preoccupied Langley, Wright, Mullaniff and Miranda Whall throughout their individual artistic and collaborative curatorial and artistic practice. In *Loop*, Langley's lozenge shaped painted panels *Limitless Play 1 & 2* mimics the intricacies of embroidery, whilst referring to abstract painting, playing optical tunes as our focus flits between various material elements in an exercise for the eyes. She writes:

> Textiles crafts have a serendipitous relationship to painting and vice versa, as iconography shuttles back and forth in either direction. This motile, capricious imagery perfectly reflects my desire to dissolve the boundaries between these traditions, to enable painting to operate within a uniquely female aesthetic. Furthermore, this craft tradition has given rise to some extraordinary works of art which should be shown alongside their 'fine art' counterparts.[57]

On the other hand, Wright's 'bead work' pattern panels, made from HAMA beads for children, pulls together an association with Op-Art and the simulacrum of a richly worked needlepoint staged against the particularities of the plastic surface. In both instances, space is trapped in a network of obsessive detail, whereby the patterning held in the panels relays the ambiguities of virtual space and the pixilation of the computer screen. In *Loop*, Wright's intervention into an elaborate Edwardian bedroom suite at Bankfield, transforms the interior of this most intimate of rooms into an uncanny, heritage tableau which further distances the viewer from any notion of an 'original' making process.[58] *Shrinking Violet*, a bedspread of beadwork, is translated into a photocopied mark; present within the image as a migrant pixel creating a continuous supply of mutant, 'hybrid' stitches crossing the borders of their proper place with alarming visual confusion in a flurry of ornamental excess. In The Pattern Lab's most recent exhibition, *Paisley: Exploding the Teardrop*, Wright takes the paisley-shaped flowerbeds of Walpole Park in London and transforms them into psychedelic imagery, from the codification of embroidery charts employed in the window graphics, to the pixilation of the paisley bhutta bead 'carpet'.[59] The significance of the construction of the rug within the home is both related to the structure of traditional Persian Garden rugs, which often bear the bhutta form and its paradisiacal potential. The 'cultivated' desert is transported into the domestic interior and is combined with Wright's more contemporary interest in the computer vitrine being the portal through which information is moved. The complex layering of horizontally-patterned carpet is based on a psychedelic bhutta; the 'portals' formed by the virtual garden details offer the viewer a continuation of movement through space. This challenges their visual logic and encourages a more physical and haptic experience in relation to its materiality. The window piece, painting and *Carpet* explore how domestic space becomes an information processor, by presenting information that hovers between virtual and material forms.

Mullaniff and Miranda Whall are both interested in the domestic space as a site for personal identification, but from different perspectives. Whall holds the view that the lace work, that was given to her by her great aunt, presented itself as an aspect of the home that was also regarded as passive".[60] She remembers that her great aunt would spend many hours at night working on tiny intricate pieces that would decorate the family home, without revealing anything of her own character. Whall's drawing mimics lace; repetitive patterns and wallpapers,

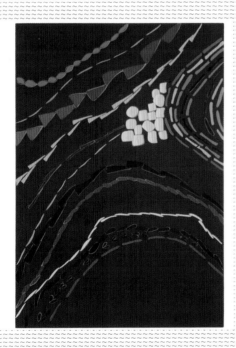

Jane Langley, *Stem, Stalk and Crewel Stitch: Silk and Ribbons*, 2006. Oil on canvas, 153 x 107 cm. Photo FXP.

referencing textile surfaces and their connotations. The complexities of process form part of her artistic strategy. Motifs are traced, scanned, arranged, digitally manipulated and then Whall hand-draws the image in her final work. Since 1994, Mullaniff has used various pictorial means within her painting practice to map and record the decorative. She has used printed fabric and floral imagery to produce several large scale rose paintings. *A Stranger to this Place,* reverberates with a sly politics that trouble any settling of the 'merely decorative' into a complex picture of muted colour and Warholian printed and painted floral patterning, *Interiors* became a series of paintings produced over eight years and inspired by a small sample of eighteenth century block printing. *Encrypted, 1–8,* 2007, follows the story of four yards of fabric which her mother bought for her in 1965 when she was seven years old.[61] These practices both take up the subject of the domestic in different ways, emphasising the traditional haptic qualities of textile in something like a common history of the female realm.

what's in a name? from expanded fields to networked interactions

What are the key questions provoked by work that refers to domestic paraphernalia, fashion victims, decorative exuberance, tartan weaves, machine knitting, recycled canvases, plastics and piles of textile stuff as stacked sculpture?

Let's remind ourselves that the notion that the extra pictorial nature of all things associated with the decorative has polluted the ways in which 'pure' abstraction is not a new criticism of textiles as fine art. Earlier in this essay I gave examples of Robert Rauschenberg's *Bed,* 1955, a painted and a quilted bedspread, the Pattern and Decoration painters of the 1970s and the broadly materialist preoccupations of Supports/Surfaces artists in France, all of whom suffered criticism from those who wished to protect 'fine art' from the threat of the decorative.

What is different now, is that the contemporary artists I have cited dismantled Greenberg's entire dictum that "decoration is the spectre that haunts modern painting".[62] "Each art form", Greenberg had declared in his essay "Modernist Painting", must determine, through a process of self-criticism "exclusive to itself".[63] It is only by limiting and narrowing down its area of competence, Greenberg reasoned, that each art form could make explicit "all that (is) unique in the nature of its medium".[64] In the paradigmatic case of painting, the essence of the medium lies in its 'ineluctable flatness' exemplified by the monochrome canvas.

How to disentangle this dilemma? What seems clear is that Greenberg claimed an autonomous self-identity for painting with reference to an outside other— whether sculpture or the applied arts—which splits or divides that identity. The move between one practice and another, a shuttling across if you will, is best exemplified, I think, by Rosalind Krauss' proposition that the production of hybrid forms and objects—neither belonging to one thing or another—blurs and disturbs categories of art practice. Consequently, she argues, such forms eclectically appropriate, replace, quote or parody, contaminate and are contaminated by 'other' traditions. She concludes, "practice is not defined in relation to any one medium but in the logical operation on a set of terms, for which any practice might be used".[65] As a consequence, the hybrid is not seen as a compound of separate parts but as a new form that is incompatible with this division, which previously defined them as separate parts. This has more unsettling repercussions, since hybrid forms and objects can succeed by showing a kaleidoscope of disparate and often colliding influences that can have disturbing implications as a result.[66]

Rosalind Krauss goes on to argue that the specificity of a medium is not to be found in its tautological self-identity but, paradoxically, in its "constitutive heterogeneity", the fact that it always differs from itself. What we are currently witnessing is the 'emigration' of textiles from itself found in the work of many contemporary artists. Has textiles become foreign to textiles? A stranger to itself (to mobilise a term from Julia Kristeva) in the sense that it is estranged from any restricted notion of textiles; no longer bounded or limited by its own self-closure or territory but open to multiple directions in form and content. As I wrote in 1995, "textile… is always 'not quite' there and also 'not quite' that… never quite settles in the same space, can never be read in the same place, in the same way twice".[67]

Hew Locke, *Golden Horde 1*, 2006.
Mixed Media—plastic (pound shop toys, Pespex, plastic flowers, sequins), metal chain, textile, on wood, 268 x 191 x 202 cm. Image courtesy of ICA and Hales Gallery, London. Photo: Marcus Leith.

Textile, its signs, practices and languages, had already shifted when I entered the debates in the mid 1970s. As I have tried to demonstrate, the 1960s and 70s had been a period of exuberance and rebellion. Textiles as a medium appeared to have no rules; it seemed to me to be naturally deconstructive, using techniques of collage and layering to manifest additive or subtractive structures with multiple referents. It proclaimed its presence by moving off the walls and becoming sculptural, painting itself into fabrics and decorative mayhem and perhaps finds its most contemporary expression in Hew Locke's *Golden Horde* mixed media installation at the ICA in 2006.[68]

In America, textiles became fibre, the change in nomenclature indicating a philosophical break with functional and industrial products, though I (like Lia Cook) now prefer the term textiles on conceptual grounds. If fibre reclaimed textiles' historical technique of quilting, stitching, printing, and fabric manipulation, it also incorporated materials that exposed any assumptions, or what had been taken as an already formed or given identity of a finite discipline. To work in the field that I have chosen has frequently been to work somewhere 'other' and as Pamela Johnson notes in her essay, "Thinking Process", to be somehow exiled:

> Perhaps we might talk not of art textiles but of art exiles. Exile can be imposed by others, but we may also choose exile; to move away from hostile, unproductive forces can be a deliberate strategy. Many key practitioners who started in the late 1960s and early 70s (such as, in this country, Janis Jefferies, Michael Brennand-Wood, Polly Binns, Caroline Broadhead) expanded their thinking beyond painting and sculpture, choosing the 'exile' in textiles rather than being forced into it. Theirs was not a wound-licking retreat but rather a regrouping in a self-determined site of investigation.[69]

In offering materials and surfaces that contain all reality that one wants or needs, textiles carry not only sensory pleasure but also a political charge and a weight of critical language. It can be something that you cannot quite put your finger on, like the tip of a needle, but it can also be as cerebral as its head. It is a broad and diffuse field, without which new modes of contemporary art practice and thinking could not flourish or survive, and which major generic forms will always flirt with, refer to and mischievously include. Contemporary art does indeed, after Duchamp, easily include textiles, but it depends where you look, and by looking, I would now use a technological term like 'searching'. Weaving, webs, holes and networks are all textile terms and mobilised within descriptions of the Internet, participatory worlds and tactile feedback. The relationship between textiles and technology is now well established and richly explored in Sadie Plant's book *Zeros + Ones* in which she insists that textiles are literally the software of all technology. It is also extraordinary to learn that Ada Lovelace, who worked with Charles Babbage on his Difference Engine, would connect the weaving of patterned silks with her own research into 'algebraic weaving'. This in turn, as we now know, led to "digital machines of the late twentieth century (that) weave new networks from what were once isolated words, numbers, music, shapes, smells, tactile textures, architectures and countless channels as yet unnamed".[70]

Weaving, Donna Harraway suggests, is for "oppositional cyborgs", whether across the computer-generated screen of satellite images or through the electronics of the loom, mindful of the politics of location in its mix of metaphors as an 'epic' tapestry' and a 'bulletin board'.[71] Others, like Charles Sherrington, Nobel-prize winning scientist researching the mind and nervous systems at the beginning of the twentieth century, called the mind "an enchanted loom where millions of flashing shuttles, weave a dissolving pattern, always a meaningful pattern though never an abiding one".[72] These metaphors, drawing textile into the fabric of technological legitimacy, are evidence of a change in perception and attitude to textile, not just in the context of art-making, but also in human culture more generally.

In *Pixel Patchwork: Quilting in Time*, Brenda Danet takes up the correspondence between 'text' and 'textile' and the fact that they share the same Latin root—*textus*, or 'woven', to describe a coloured form of text-based art that finds expression in ASC11 art (pronounced AS-kee). ASC11 can be traced back to the 1970s. Since the advent of Windows 95, participants in certain channels (or chat rooms) on a popular chat mode called IRC (Internet Relay Chat) play with patterns and play off ornament in abundant colour pixels to produce variations on 'quilting in time', rather than space. Danet emphasises how an on-line group called Rainbow mobilise complex computer skills rather than those that are more materially-focused.[73] Everyone using these channels can use images created by others as 'token for interactions'. Colour combinations and reformations no longer rely on research laboratories; each colour can be so modified and mutated that the participants can ask: is this the colour blue? In Danet's view the computer screen relays new

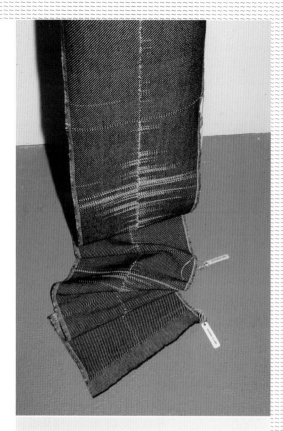

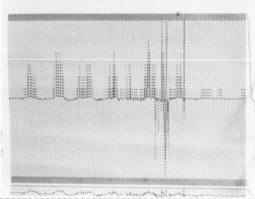

TOP TO BOTTOM

Ingrid Bachmann & Barbara Layne, *Fault Lines: Measurement, Distance and Place*, 1995.
Detail of Computer Loom, La Centrale Galerie, Montreal, Quebec. Photo: Paul Litherland.

Ingrid Bachmann & Barbara Layne, *Fault Lines: Measurement, Distance and Place*, 1995.
Translation of seismograph into weave structure, 21.6 x 27.9 cm. Street Projects, Santa
Monica, California. Photo: Barbara Layne.

forms of art works but both offer new ways of imaging new subjectivities—plugged in and downloaded—readings and practices in which disparate voices interact and intersect between a network of spaces, texts and pattern.

Ingrid Bachman explore some of these implications in her interactive installation, *Knit One/Swim 2*, first shown in the *Presence of Touch* exhibition at the School of the Art Institute in Chicago during 1996. We are engaged in a strange yet bodily encounter with a gigantic pair of steel knitting needles, each nearly four metres long and suspended from the ceiling. The action is translated into a notation system and the construction of a digital image. The viewer can manipulate the needles and, as they are operated, weights which help suspend them, are dipped into powdered pigment and leave marks on an adjacent wall. The movement of the weights is tracked by a sensor system, and the information is then fed into a computer screen. The knitting is created 'virtually'. These, and other new conceptual configurations of textile, evidence surprising and complex models for understanding the place of material in the future of fine art.

As produced in collaboration with Barbara Layne, *Fault Lines: Measurement, Distance and Place* embrace a relationship between a material and notational form. In this key work from the 1990s, computer-assisted looms are programmed to translate daily-recorded seismographic readings between two distinct locations and two different exhibition places: Montreal and Santa Monica. Volunteer weavers came on a daily basis to the two sites geographically distinct, each individual weaving part of the fabric in response to the tectonic movements of the earth monitored through the internet and translated by specially designed software. The simultaneous production of the two fabrics record, measure and transform information into a woven record of time, the weavers' bodies (the shifting rhythms of their hand movements in the weaving process) and the seismographic data collected. I first saw part of the piece at La Centrale as part of the satellite exhibitions that accompanied the *Textile Sismographs* colloquia in Montreal during 1995 (it was re-staged at *Presence of Touch* exhibition at the School of the Art Institute, Chicago during 1996). It is an extraordinary work, which functions through its own dynamic, feeding back into the processes by which it is made through loops within itself. As a hand-made artefact and as a technologically generated representation, *Fault Lines* brings an updated version of the 'art fabric' (as once conceived by Constantine and Larsen) into a world of new investigations and interconnections, between the haptic and aesthetic surfaces of material structure, the simulated and the digital.

In summary, the very material of textiles has itself become electronic equipment. The responsive textile surface serves as a carrier of thought, as Suzanne Kuchler suggests in her essay, "Re-thinking Textile: The Advent of the 'Smart' Fiber Surface".[74] We are pushed to think in terms of associations that are no longer unique but are couched in the materiality of the thing within which the image dwells. The secret apparently lies in the knitted pattern of the fibres, which, when touched, determines how the electrical signals pass through it, revealing how contact was made with the material. With the new Fibre Optic Animated Motion technology, it becomes possible to shimmer white lights onto evening gowns, animate facial features on the surface of a child's back-pack, insert glowing lights into the fabric of camping tents. This results in a dazzling display on the surface of fabric thanks to a propriety process for permanently bonding the fibres to certain soft and pliable surfaces. In the field of smart textiles, anything would now appear to be possible. It challenges our notion of a relationship to a world of things, the subtle physical sensations between substances and surface, once known through our relationship to skin. Touch, the interplay of the senses, comes into power on the web, our interaction with it and an examination of the relationship between the material and the immaterial. As Sadie Plant points out:

> The digital revolution is unleashing an entirely new set of paradigms and perspectives for the future—involving cybernetic, non-linear processes which cut across and interconnect all areas of material life. The processes of spinning, plaiting and weaving have been imperceptibly changing the world, finally emerging as the digitisation of reality, and as new possibilities of matter to interconnect and engineer itself in unprecedented patterns and new designs. As both male and female practitioners increasingly work with computerised looms, intelligent fabrics, pixelled screens, and the Internet, this connection between sexes, textiles, and technical process are converging as never before.[75]

To conclude, we live in exciting times, full of new material possibilities and technological innovation. Textiles are at the very vanguard of contemporary art practices and social change today. They are now seen as the material culture of the future, with the potential to transform the way we think, live and behave in an ever-increasing networked culture where our bodies ache and our gestures twitch with an excitable, physical determination to remake and make anew.

1. Jefferies, Janis, "The Development and Role of Soft Material in British Painting and Sculpture and the Textiles Arts", *The Textile Society Newsletter for the Study of Textile Art, Design and Theory*, No. 4, Autumn 1985, pp 7–19.

2. Constantine, Mildred and Jack Lenor Larsen, *The Art Fabric Mainstream*, toured America under the American Federation of Arts opening at the San Francisco Museum of Art, May 21–July 5,1981.

3. Constantine, Mildred and Jack Lenor Larsen, *Beyond Craft: The Art Fabric*, New York: Van Nostrand Reinhold, 1973, p 12.

4. Boccioni, Umberto. "Technical Manifesto of Futurist Sculpture", in *Theories of Modern Art*, Herscel Chipp ed., Berkeley: University of California Press, 1968, p 304.

5. Seiz, Peter, "Knots and Bolts", *Art in America*, Vol. 70, No. 2, February 1982, p 107.

6. Constantine, *The Art Fabric Mainstream*.

7. For a further analysis on craft and its complex histories, see, Admason, Glenn, *Thinking through Craft*, Oxford: Berg Publishing/Victoria and Albert Museum, 2007. John Houston ed, *Craft Classics: An Anthology of Belief and Comment*, London: Crafts Council, 1988. Tanya Harrod, *The Crafts in Britain in the Twentieth Century*, Yale: Yale University Press, 1999. This book accompanied an exhibition of British crafts, *The Pleasures of Peace: Craft, Art and Design in Britain from the 1940s to the 1960s*, that opened at the Sainsbury Centre at the University of East Anglia in Spring,1999.

8. The most significant exhibition, and one which monitored and provided a platform for the art fabric or textile avant-garde, was the international Lausanne Biennial which was organised by the Musée des Beaux Arts, Lausanne, Switzerland from 1962 until 1995. I religiously visited and wrote reviews of the exhibition from 1977 until 1977, for British, and Australian textile journals. It was the only occasion in Europe for seeing the pioneers of the is mostly a forgotten phenomenon but the impact of the enormous fibre-based installations of Magdalena Abakanowiz, Jagoda Buic, Peter and Ritzi Jacobi, Sheila Hicks, Olga de Amaral, Ursula Plewka-Schmidt and Daniel Graffin left an indelible impression. For a history of the Lausanne Biennials, see Janis Jefferies and Angele Ruchti Ruchti, exhibition guide for *Textile Art: Textiles from the Collection of the Pierre Pauli Association and the Lausanne Biennial*, Switzerland, Salts Mill, Bradford, Britain, 1 April–17 June, 1990. It was the first time that any of the works from the Biennial had been shown in Britain. The exhibitions was organised as part of the *Textile Arts Festival* in Bradford, 1990. The last and sixteenth Lausanne Biennial, Parallel Histories, was held in the summer of 1995. It offered a comparative history of some 20 works illustrating textile art of the last 30 years. Contemporary artists who used the same type of materials staged these works with 20 pieces. A felt by Beuys, some kilims by Alighiero E Boetti, a coat by Etienne-Marrin, a stack by Flanagan, a wall of rags by Pistoletto and a glove by Rebecca Horn. There were two large *Abakans* by Magdalena Abakanowicz, some horsehair writing by Pierrette Bloch, a wardrobe of clothes by Ritzi Jacobi, some grills by Karen Hansen, a black environment by Naomi Kobayashi and an ethereal composition by Elsi Giauque.

9. Thomas, Michael, "10th Lausanne Biennial", *Crafts Magazine*, November/December 1981 pp 24–27.

10. Sorkin, Jenni, "Way Beyond Craft: Thinking through the Work of Mildred Constantine", *Textile: The Journal of Cloth and Culture*, Oxford: Berg Publishing, vol 1, issue 1, March 2003, p 44. I provided the images for the essay based on my visits to the international Lausanne Biennial.

11. Morris, Linda, *Cut, Folded & Tied*, and catalogue essay on Richard Smith, London: Arts Council of Great Britain,1975.

12. Iverson, Margaret, *Alos Reigel*, Cambridge and London: MIT Press, 1996.

13. Wood, Brennand Michael, *Fabric and Form: New Textile Art from Britain*, London: A British Council and Crafts Council catalogue, 1982, p 5.

14. Parker, Rozika and Griselda Pollock, *Old Mistresses: Women, Art and Ideology*, London: Routledge & Kegan Paul, 1981.

15. Parker, Rozika, "Old Mistresses: Women, Art and Ideology"

16. Huyseen, Andreas, *After the Great Divide: Modernism, Mass Culture, Postmodernism*, Bloomington: Indiana University Press, 1986, p 55.

17. Greenberg, Clement, "Clement Greenberg: The Collected Essay and Criticism", *Modernism with a Vengeance*, Vol. 4,1957–1969, John O'Brian ed., London: University of Chicago Press, 1993.

18. Greenberg, Clement, cited in Christopher Reed's introduction to *Not at Home: The Suppression of Modern Art and Architecture*, London: Thames and Hudson, 1996. p 15.

19. Reed, *Not at Home*, p 15.

20. Jefferies, Janis, "Yinka Shonibare: Dressing Down Textiles in a Victorian Philanthropists Parlour", in *Re -Inventing Textiles: Tradition and Innovation*, Vol. 1, Sue Rowley ed., Winchester: Telos Art Publishing, 1999, p 65.

21. Schor, Naomi, *Reading in Detail: Aesthetics and the Feminine*, London: Methuen,1987.

22. Loos, Adolf, *Ornament and Crime: Selected Essays: Adolf Loos*, selected and introduced by Adolf Opel, Michael Mitchell trans., Riverside, California: Adriane Press,1998.

23. Carter, Michael, *Putting a Face on Things: Studies in the Imaginary Materials*, Sydney: Power Publication, 1997, pp 118–120.

24. During the 1990s, there was an abundant flowering of handiwork and craft as well as textile-based processes notably mobilising stitch, whether as metaphor for tactility and sexuality, see Tracey Emin's *Bed*, 1998, or as blended examples of western fashion hybridised with African ethnicity to create abstracted replicants, Enrico David's work in the *New Labour* exhibition, Saatchi Gallery, London, 2001. See my "Loving Attention: an Outburst of Craft in Contemporary Art", paper delivered at the School of the Art Institute of Chicago, America, on

10 October 2007 as part of the Object of Labor public talks. The paper will be published in essay form as part of the anthology, *Extra/ordinary: Craft culture and Contemporary Art*, edited by Maria Buszek for Duke University Press in summer 2008.

25. Jefferies, Janis, *Boys Who Sew*, exhibition leaflet for exhibition of same title, Crafts Council and touring 2004–2005.

26. Corns, M. and R. Nickas, "Punishment and Decoration: Art in an Age of Militant Superficiality", *Artforum*, 31, no 8, April 1983, p 83. The full quote strongly suggests that decoration and embellishment can generate complex visual malapropisms. Further discussion of this issue can be found in the exhibition catalogue, *Warped: Painting and the Feminine*, Angel Row Gallery, Nottingham, Britain, pp 4–16. The exhibition was held between 20 January and 10 March 2001, and featured the work of Jo Bruton alongside that of Valerie Jaudon.

27. Meyer, Melissa and Miriam Schapiro, "Waste Not/Want Not: Femmage", *Heresies: Feminist Publication on Art and Politics*, Winter, 1978, pp 66–69.

28. Nochlin, Linda and Miriam Schapiro, *Shaping the Fragments of Art and Life*, New York: Harry N Abrams and Polk Museum of Art, 1999, p 8.

29. Goldin, Amy, "Patterns Grids and Paintings". *Artforum*, Vol. 14, No. 1, September, 1975.

30. Rickey, Carrie, "Decoration, Ornament, Pattern and Utility: Four Tendencies in Search of a Movement", Giancorio Politi and Helena Kontova eds, *Flash Art: Two Decades of History XX1 Years*, Milan: MIT Press, 1990, pp 59–61.

31. Perreault, John, "Issues in Pattern Painting", *Artforum*, Vol. 16, No. 3, November 1977, p33.

32. Perreault, John, "Issues in Pattern Painting", *Artforum*, Vol 16, November 1977, p 34.

33. Perreault, John. "Issues in Pattern Painting", *Artforum*, Vol 16, November 1977, p 36.

34. Kingsley, April, "Opulent Optimism," *Village Voice*, 28 November, 1977, cited in Broude, "The Pattern and Decoration Movement," in *The Power of Feminist Art: The American Movement of the 1970s, History and Impact*, Norma and Garrard D Mary eds, New York: Harry N Abrams, 1994, pp 212–13.

35. *Ten Approaches to the Decorative*, Allesandra Gallery, 25 September–29 October, 1976 included Valerie Jaudon, Joyce Kozloff, Miriam Schapiro and Robert Zakanych.

36. Perone, Jeff, "Approaching the Decorative", *Artforum*, December 1976, p 28.

37. Perone, Jeff, "The Decorative Impulse," *Artforum*, November 1979, pp 80–81.

38. *Heresies: A Feminist Publication on Art and Politics* on "Women's Traditional Arts: The Politics of Aesthetics", 1978. The special issue also includes essays by Melissa Meyer and Miriam Schapiro, "Waste Not/Want Not: Femmage" and Linda Nochlin, "Excerpts from Women and the Decorative Arts".

39. Shonibare, Yinka, *Maxa 2003*, emulsion, acrylic on textile, 74 panels. *Maxa* was shown at the Turner Prize exhibition, Tate Britain, 2004. It is now in the collection of Melva Bucksbaum and Raymond Learsy, America.

40. Yinka Shonibare, interview with the author, London, February 1998. Other quotes are also from this interview, unless given a specific reference.

41. Chave, Anna C, cites Carrie Rickey on this aspect of Jaudon's work. See, Chave's essay, "Disorderly Order: The Art of Valerie Joudan" for *Valerie Jaudon: a Retrospective*, Mississippi Museum of Art, 24 May–3 August 1996, Mississippi: University Press of Mississippi, 1996.

42. Gombrich, EH, "The Sense of Order", quoted by Anna C Chave in "Disorderly Order: The Art of Valerie Jaudon", 1996, p 39.

43. Gombrich, EH, *The Sense of Order*, New York: Cornell University Press, 1979.

44. Kraft, Selma, "Cognitive Function and Women's Art", *Women's Art Journal*, Vol. 4, No. 2 Autumn 1983/Winter 1984, pp 5–9.

45. Admason makes a persuasive argument in thinking through craft, that although "there were various attempts to legitimise the move in theoretical terms, notably on the part of Perrone, whose familiarity with Derrida's notion of the supplement is evident both in his arguments and in his elliptical writing style". He takes a particular passage of Perone's writing to observe that: "Decoration, he wrote in 1980 both beside and beyond, near and amiss (Para- of the paradigm is neither the inside nor outside, but the frame and the border, the para- of the decorative confusion of an adorned outside of cloth and an ornamented inside.. .)." Sadly, Admason goes on to say that, "this argument never coalesced an accepted critical account of the Movement. Commentary on Pattern and Decoration art instead revolved around ill-defined attempts to connect it to early modern instances of pictorial arbitrariness and exoticism, such as the paintings of Matisse". See, Admason, Glenn, *Thinking through Craft*, Oxford: Berg Publishing/Victoria and Albert Museum, 2007, p 32.

46. See Pagel, David, "Polly Apfelbaum: Ring-A-Ring-Roses", *Art+Text*, No. 53, January, 1996, pp 48–54 and David Pagel, "Jim Iserman/Best of Both Worlds", *Art+Text*, No. 57, May–July, 1997, pp 66–54.

47. *Every Touch* was produced in collaboration with The Fabric Workshop and Museum (FWM). FWN was founded in 1977 by Marion Boulton Stroud and is the only non-profit arts organisation in America devoted to creating new work in new materials and new media in collaboration with emerging, nationally, and internationally recognised artists. The FWM Museum collection now has over 5,500 objects created by more than 400 artists who have participated in the artist-in-residency programme. For further information on FWM, see Anne Bourbeau. "New Material as New Media: The Fabric Workshop and Museum" in *Textile: The Journal of Cloth and Culture*, vol 1, no 3, 1 September 2003, Oxford: Berg Publishing, pp 302–305.

48. Perle, Nadia, "Simon Hantai", *Driadi/Textile Art*, No. 16, 1981, pp 4–8. *Driadi/Textile Art* was an influential journal published in French and edited by Michel Thomas in Paris. It was the only journal that explored issues in all fields of contemporary visual and material practice. It ceased publication in 1989.

49. Les Années Supports/Surfaces dans les collections du Centre Georges Pompidou was shown at the Galerie Nationale du Jeu de Paume, Paris, and 19 May–30 August 1998. Further discussion around the artists shown can be found at "Supports/Surfaces: Contexts and Issues" by Mick Finch for the Supports/Surfaces: Critiques of Modernism conference paper given at Courtauld Institute, London, Britain, 27 February 1999.

50. *Pattern Crazy, Crafts Council Gallery*, London, Britain, 4 July–1 September 2002.

51. Louise Taylor quoted in Albert Hill's "Design: A Question of Taste", *Independent*, 29 June 2002.

52. Camden Arts Centre, London, showed Simon Periton from 11 December–31 January 1999, Jim Isermann from 16 July–29 August 1999, Laura Ford and Jacqui Poncelet: *A Stranger Here Myself*, 11 December–31 January 1999 and Yinka Shonibare, 16 June–20 July 2000.

53. Rickey, Claire, "Decorating, Ornament, Pattern and Utility: Four Tendencies in Search of a Movement", in *Flash Art: Two Decades of History XX1 Years*, Giancorio Politi and Helena Kontova eds, Milan: MIT Press, 1990, p 61.

54. Jefferies, Janis, "Touching Material, Reading in Detail", catalogue essay for Lia Cook: *Material Allusions*, Oakland: Oakland Museum of California, pp15–20.

55. Danto, C Arthur, "Reflections on Fabric and Meaning: The Tapestry and the Loin Cloth", in *New Material as New Message: The Fabric Museum and Workshop*, ed Marion Boulton Stroud, Cambridge, MA: MIT Press, pp 82–89.

56. Saunders, Gill, *Purl*, 2004, catalogue essay which can be accessed through The Pattern Lab website, www.thepatternlab.com.

57. Artist statement submitted to the author, November 2007.

58. The bed in the Edwardian room at Bankfield was donated by the Murgatroyd family in the 1960s. Similar to the Ackroyd family before them, their wealth was also made through the textile industry.

59. *Paisley: Exploding the Teardrop*, PM Gallery & House, 16 November 2007–19 January 2008. In collaboration with The Pattern Lab, the show explores the roots of paisley—its origins, development over the centuries and the myriad uses to which it has been put. The artists include Laurie Addis, Lisa Busby, Jane Langley, Delaine Le Bas, Kathleen Mullaniff, Rekha Rodwittiya, Gurdeep Sehmar and Jennifer Wright.

60. Whall, proposal for Bankfield Museum subsequently sent to the author, July 2002.

61. Jefferies, Janis, "Patterning Attention" catalogue essay for Kathleen Mullaniff: *Traces*, pp 4–8. The exhibition was held at Wolsey Art Gallery, Christchurch Mansion, Ipswich, 11 January –7 March 2004.

62. On Yinka Shonibare, see my essay "Dressing Down Textiles in a Victorian Philanthropists Parlour" in *Re -Inventing Textiles: Tradition and Innovation*, Sue Rowley ed., Vol. 1, Winchester: Telos Art Publishing, 1999, pp 59–73.

63. Greenberg, Clement, "Modernist Painting", in *Clement Greenberg: the Collected Essays and Criticism*, John O'Brian ed., Vol. 4 Chicago: University of Chicago Press, 1986, p 86.

64. Greenberg, "Modernist Painting", p 86.

65. Krauss, Rosalind, *Sculpture in the Expanded Field*, Chicago: MIT Press, 1979, pp 31–41.

66. For further reading of hybrid forms, questions of hybridity and contemporary art, see Nikos Papastergiadis, "Restless Hybrids", and Judy Purdom, "Mapping Difference" in *Third Text*, No. 32, Autumn 1995, pp 9–19, 19–23.

67. Jefferies, Janis, "Textile Identity", in *Textile Sismographs, Symposium Fibres et Textiles—Texts from the Colloquim*, Montreal: Counseil des arts textiles du Quebec, 1995, pp 20–28.

68. Locke, Hew, Golden Horde, and seven pieces of various sizes, commissioned by ICA and inIVA for inclusion in the exhibition *Alien Nation* at the ICA, 17 November 2006–14 January 2007.

69. Johnson, Pamela, "Thinking Process", catalogue to *Arttextiles*, the second major survey of British artists working with textiles, Bury St Edmunds Gallery, 2000, p 21. As Johnson notes, work by Janis Jefferies from the 1980s and 1990s was shown at the Norwich Art Gallery, 6 October–12 November 2000 with an accompanying anthology of Jefferies' critical writing, called *Selvedges*, 1980–2000; see also Brennand-Wood, Michael: *You Are Here*, Hare Print Press, 1999; PhD Thesis by Polly Binns, "Vision and Process in Textile Art" housed in the of University of Teesside, Buckinghamshire Chilterns University College and The British Library, also in the Art Gallery Manchester and Crafts Council, London; *Bodyscape: Caroline Broadhead*, published by Angel Row Gallery, Nottingham/Northern Gallery for Contemporary Art, Sunderland on the occasion of the exhibition of the same title, 1999.

70. Plant, Sadie, *Zeros+Ones, Digital Women + The New Technoculture*, London: Fourth Estate, 1998, p 23.

71. Jefferies, Janis. in "Text and Textiles: Weaving Across the Borderlines" ed Katy Deepwell, *Towards New Feminist Criticism: Critical Strategies*, pp 164–175.

72. McCormack, John, "Unweaving Complexity", *Craft*, the magazine of Craft Australia, vol 32, no 241, 2001, p 19.

73. Danet, Brenda. "Pixel Patchwork: Quilting in Time", in *Textile: The Journal of Cloth and Culture*, Vol. 1, No. 3, 1 September 2003, Oxford: Berg Publishing pp 118–143.

74. Kuchler, Suzanne, "Re-Thinking Textiles: The Advent of the 'Smart' Fiber Surface" in *Textile: The Journal of Cloth and Culture*, Vol. 1, No. 3, 1 September 2003, Oxford: Berg Publishing, pp 262–272.

75. Plant, Sadie, "Lady Ada, Queen of Engines", *Textile Sismographs, Symposium fibres et textiles—Texts from the Colloquim*, Montreal: Counseil des arts textiles du Quebec, 1995, p 110.

DRAW

VINGS

Andrea Dezsö, *Lessons from my Mother*. Embroidery, various threads on white cotton canvas. Image courtesy of the artist.

Andrea Dezsö

Andrea Dezsö was born in Transylvania. Brought up in the communist regime, she moved to New York in 1997. Despite the stark contrast between communist Transylvania and New York, the 'city that never sleeps' was an inspiring contrast to her homeland. Through her work, Dezsö began questioning the application of the rules of her old country in modern-day North America, famed for its own system of codes, weaving a deeply personal narrative between her multinational experiences.

~~~~~ Having been exposed to the samplers found in the Hungarian kitchens of her childhood, Dezsö noted their dual protective functions—espousing physical safety and cautionary tale, itself a form of social protection. Mimicking their style, she chose to incorporate the family superstition she had been taught

as fact into her embroidered pieces. Each piece, beginning with the embroidered words "My Mother Claimed That", depicts a cautionary proverb, accompanied by an often crude and surprising pictorial representation. Many of the images appear to reference medical journal imagery—a style that directly affronts the 'wisdom' being depicted on the pictural plane and becomes a playful antidote to the serious claims being made.

~~~~~ It is this juxtaposition of several different elements—anatomical imagery, rendered harmless in a tactile thread medium and depicting impossible, absurd tales—which acts as the core of the work. These elements merge seamlessly together to form a coherent series, alarming, unusual and humourous. The playful piece *Our Nanny had Six Puppy Dogs Sewn into her Stomach by her*

Andrea Dezsö, *Lessons from my Mother*.
Embroidery, various threads on white cotton canvas. Image courtesy of the artist.

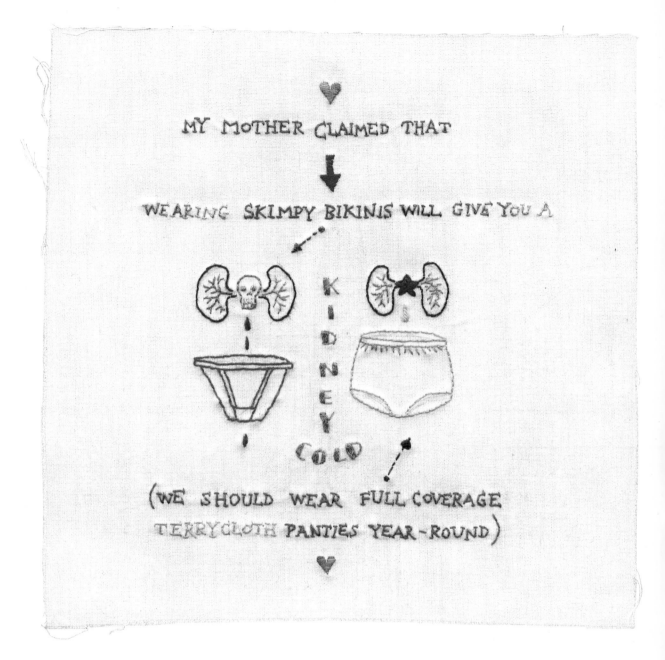

MY MOTHER CLAIMED THAT

WEARING SKIMPY BIKINIS WILL GIVE YOU A

K
I
D
N
E
Y

COLD

(WE SHOULD WEAR FULL COVERAGE
TERRYCLOTH PANTIES YEAR-ROUND)

Previous Employer is a prime example of the way in which a serious claim becomes a comic burst through Dezsö's representation. Though the tales expressed in Dezsö's work are difficult to believe, we become wide-eyed before them, suspending disbelief and entering the theatre of cultural meanings she expresses through her nearly childlike representations.

The sacred notion of virginity and sexual promiscuity is examined by Dezsö in pieces like *If you Let a Man Fuck you he'll Leave you Because Every Man Wants to Marry a Virgin*. We, as viewers, don't necessarily believe the dictum, but can't help but hear the distant echo of voices from our own cultural histories. This mother-knows-best attitude to life is simultaneously exulted and ridiculed as we all recognise the sentiment behind these works, even if we do not subscribe to the content. Dezsö takes up the myth of her cultural heritage and employs a visual language that is suggestive of the folk theory it espouses, but frames it within a contemporary context that lays bare the meanings and connotations of her subject and method.

OPPOSITE: Annie Whiles, *Bad Chair Day*.
Embroidered badge, canvas, felt, satin and embroidery silks, 50 x 50 cm. Image courtesy of the artist.

Annie Whiles, *Hover Boys*.
Embroidery, canvas, felt, satin and embroidery silks, 50 x 50 cm. Image courtesy of the artist.

Annie Whiles

Everyday objects are invested with a grand importance in Annie While's embroidery. Intricately constructed from layers of canvas, felt, satin and silk, the familiar objects we surround ourselves with each day, take on a mythical quality. Chairs, tables, cutlery, make-up, even neighbours and matches are transformed into icons of the world we inhabit. The ordinary becomes the extraordinary, or, as Bernard Walsh describes it, "the drawings represent nothing and plenty more besides".[1]

~~~~~ Children often grow up with a series of badges representing personal achievements, as is common in child institutions such as the Brownies or Boy Scouts. Sewn onto sashes or sleeves, these badges become emblems of what we take to be important or useful skills each boy or girl should be taught, necessary for their very survival in some cases. These childhood versions of

honorific icons find their adult equivalent in the military system, where particularly important skills are branded on the very body of the person who possesses them. Whiles takes up the ideology surrounding badges—cultural signifiers of accomplishment and worth—and imbues them with alternate meanings, highlighting their very function as a social language and system of hierarchy. These are not simply straightforward depictions of useful or socially significant skills, ranks or qualities. Rather, they are metaphors for emotionally or socially significant situations or experiences. Whiles' badges seem to elaborate the trials that come with adulthood, and the experiences gained in dealing with them. These works offer humourous studies of everyday human behaviour and frustration presented to us as motifs, rendered significant through

their framing. The piece, *Bad Chair Day* is a subversion of the minor anxiety concerning a bad hair day and plays with the idea that even one of life's miniscule complications can become immortalised as an icon of experience. As Bernard Walsh observes: "Often the subjects chosen have an amazing starting point. Not because they are, within themselves, anything extraordinary or unique in terms of proposition or perspective but because they are very ordinary".[2] The viewer is invited to consider their own everyday experiences as worthy of acknowledgement, perhaps even exaltation.

Whiles deploys ambiguous signifiers in many of her pieces, at times nearly mythical, as in *Bad Chair Day*'s bucket-carrying monkeys, or Hover Boys bird-headed men. The meaning of these signifiers is not immediately given to the viewer, rather the mythical connotations opens up the possibility of reading the work as metaphor, fable or cautionary tale. Whiles' work stimulates the very human need to search, study and rationalise elements from our own experience and culture, and from something like the collective imagination.

1. Walsh, Bernard, Exhibition pamphlet for Annie Whiles' *Cuckoo* at Danielle Arnaud Gallery, 9 March–15 April 2007.
2. Walsh, Bernard, Exhibition pamphlet for Annie Whiles' *Cuckoo*.

OPPOSITE: Jessica Rankin, *Passage (Dusty Humming)*, 2007. Embroidery on organdy, 108 x 151 cm. Image courtesy Jay Jopling/White Cube, London.

Jessica Rankin, *Coda*, 2004. Embroidery on organdy, 193 x 111.8 cm. Image courtesy of the artist and The Project, New York.

Jessica Rankin

Jessica Rankin's work features a languorous and ethereal collection of imagery infused with equal parts of the mystical and the technical. Her work is built from layers and layers of delicate fabrics, cartographic forms and poetic embroideries, giving rise to an otherworldly, hazy visual world that is at once beautiful and thought-provoking.

~~~~~ Rankin uses organdy fabric as the base material for the work, taking swatches of the material and blending them together in visually complex and exciting palettes, often culminating in mural-sized works of art. Her palettes range in colour from softly muted earth tones and diaphanous whites, to deep indigos and crimsons, all presented in an absolute lightness that seems to lift off the wall and into the very air of the gallery space. In Rankin's work, the organdy—a fabric that was commonly used in Victorian dressmaking—is appropriated and transformed into an ethereal medium upon which multiple signifiers are woven together in a series of compelling visual narratives. Although the artist works in what has been a traditionally feminine medium, she draws upon cartography, astronomy and genetic mapping as sources of inspiration, fusing two conceptually gendered worlds. The loose threads of her embroidery, set against the provocative content of her words and the elusive material background of her 'canvas', create a sense of the incomplete or the unrealised.

~~~~~ Rankin expresses her preference for the aesthetic of the surreal with the visual construction of her works, but also in the naming of them. Titles such as *Hinterland*, 2007, and *Nocturne*, 2004, are suggestive of a mystical natural

landscape upon where the creative imaginary is played out. Working almost as a poet of imagery, Rankin's awareness of language resonates throughout her work. In *Nocturne* her stream-like verse softly mumbles "ANENDLESSRELEASEOFLANGUAGE" over the surface of the organdy. In *Hour to Hour,* 2007, the cartographic references stitched into the fabric mingle with zigzags of language atop the tan, green, and white organdy, with details mimicking a double-helix wind in between the layers of material. *Passage (Dusty Humming),* 2007, is a deviation from Rankin's characteristic cartographic form in that the work consists of one continuous word sewn as a paragraph, covering the entire surface of the organdy canvas. The *Passage* evokes the language of the unconscious in one endless and breathless thought that grows bolder and softer with its passage.

~~~~~ The experience of these works is often surreal, echoing the fleeting emotions, senses and desires of fever or half-sleep. Rankin deploys compelling visual elements that are played out on a large scale, positioning the viewer in an ambiguous landscape somewhere between consciousness and unconsciousness, thinking and saying and softness and depth.

OPPOSITE: Karen Reimer, *prime number pillow cases*, 2007. Embroidery on cotton. Image courtesy of the artist and Monique Meloche Gallery. Photo: Tom Van Eynde.

Karen Reimer, *prime number pillow cases*, 2007. Embroidery on cotton. Image courtesy of the artist and Monique Meloche Gallery. Photo: Tom Van Eynde.

Karen Reimer

Chicago-based Karen Reimer calls herself a craft-based conceptual artist, making work that "examines the relationships between beauty, value and meaning by exploiting the tensions between copy and original, object and process and fine art and domestic craft".[1]

~~~~~ She invariably uses the medium of sewing in her work, decorating pillowcases, stitching together a variety of fabric that express diverse social connotations, overlaying found sewing patterns to create textile-based text or reproducing newspaper cut-outs in a textile medium.

~~~~~ Reimer studied at both Bethel College in Kansas and the University of Chicago in the 1980s and, in the past two decades, has built up an extremely diverse visual language in her practice. In addition to her text pieces she has recently started making installation works, where hanging fabrics take the form of scrolls positioned in sequence on the wall. Her installation work often includes decorative pieces, such as cushions for example, often blurring the boundaries between craft and fine art, and encouraging a wider definition of high culture that might include craft or the ornamental.

~~~~~ Reimer plays with notions of value and originality by creating works that are at the once laboriously and skillfully produced, and (often incomplete or inaccurate) reproductions of unremarkable or familiar artefacts. Through her creative method, Reimer alters these reproductions sufficiently to support her claim that they are in fact 'originals', taking up debates about authorship and appropriation. The notions of value and perspective are elaborated through

Reimer's choice of subject, often selecting pieces of waste as the starting point for her working method.

Many of her text works appear incomplete, as though something has been lost in the translation between the original images and Reimer's reproduction of them. Numbers and letters are missing, leaving the viewer to guess at what comes next, or what came before. These images become signifiers in their own right, emblems of the way in which we process information—a letter here, an image there—merged in the human consciousness to make a forced legible whole. These tricks of consciousness play off of the more literal symbols of Reimer's choice of subject and form, encouraging a critical look at what might be forced categories of craft and fine art, or worth and waste.

1. From the artist's statement, submitted to the author in November 2007.

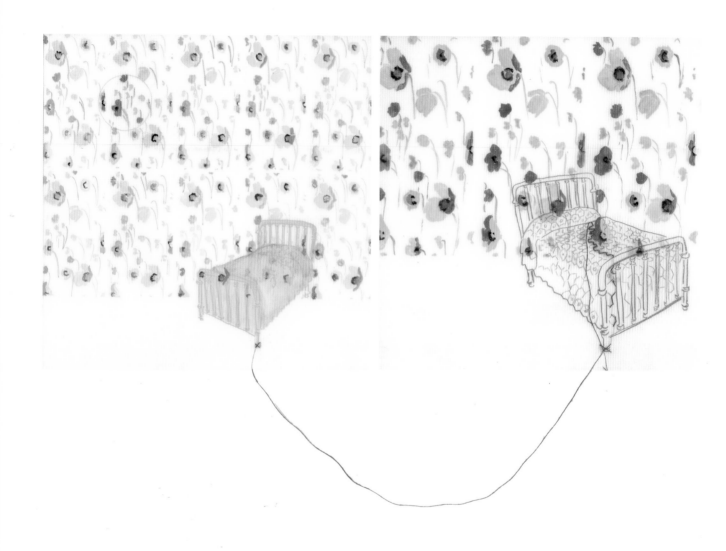

Lisa Solomon

Through her multi-media work, Lisa Solomon takes up the traditional language of the feminine and rearticulates it in wholly surprising ways, rendering the original meaning of domestic artefacts absurd through the dialogue of her work.
~~~~~ Working predominantly in the realm of the domestic, Solomon performs the repetitive, mundane actions associated with women's work to great effect, radicalising these actions through a change of context and narrative. Sewing without thread is one such technique, where Solomon appropriates a perfectly reasonable domestic chore and chips away at its meaning, leaving only a series of perforations where the maternal remit of binding and mending should be. Oftentimes Solomon will take decidedly masculine, at times aggressive, subject matter and build her representation from feminine, pliable, comfortable materials, as in her bright pink-felted tanks, or her embroidered Mitsubishi A6M Zero fighter planes.
~~~~~ Solomon not only works with the method associated with household chores, but also often chooses household objects as her subject, creating vibrant embroidery work depicting things like chairs, beds or clothing. She often leaves long strings hanging from these works, or presents them in reverse to reveal the working side of the piece, suggestive of process and creating an intimacy with the work as an object in the world.
~~~~~ Solomon's use of textiles runs a logical streak through her work, binding together her choice of subject in form in a fluid, changeable material, fundamentally linked with the domestic realm she cleaves open with her visually exciting method.

Rachel Coleman, *New York*, 2007.
Hand and machine embroidery, Mixed media, 15 x 25 cm.

OPPOSITE: Lisa Solomon, *poppybed*, 2007.
Watercolor, coloured pencil, thread/embroidery on Duralar, 45.7 x 20.3 cm.

Rachel Coleman

British artist Rachel Coleman manipulates fabric cutouts, safety pins, wool and buttons to produce charmingly naive textile-based collages. Her subject matter often takes up imagery one might find in a children's book, such as rabbits, seagulls, donkeys, or playgrounds, drawing inspiration from everyday life, the urban landscape and the nostalgia of childhood trips to the British seaside.
~~~~~ She uses the sewing machine to draw freely on the canvas, stitching fluid lines to create block areas of colour alongside her stark applications of collaged imagery. Coleman generates layer upon layer of material, embellished with everyday materials such as zips, hooks, paper clips and straight pins. Coleman displays a confident use of pattern, texture and colour, deploying a variety of working methods that range from printing to embroidery and appliqué.

The resulting work is a riot of signifiers, with an application that is as brutal as it is playful. "Historically", Coleman claims, "embroidery has been used as a method to convey everyday life experiences using mundane and domestic imagery. Within my work I try to reference this by using old techniques such as applique, hand-embroidery and stump work alongside modern visual images."[1] Though Coleman uses what she takes to be the language of the mundane or familiar, her works are rendered shocking through bold use of colour and form.

~~~~~~

1. Taken from the artist's statement, submitted to the author in November 2007.

Orly Cogan, Green Haze.
Hand-stitched embroidery on vintage linen, 127 x 109.2 cm.

Orly Cogan

Orly Cogan's work ranges from two-dimensional wall pieces to installations and photography, exploring the conventions of femininity through stitching into vintage fabrics. Her pieces are like pages of a sketchbook full of life drawings, which Cogan explores through more contrived compositions verging on fantasy. Embroidered female forms interact with each other and discreet objects, exploring feminine archetypes such as the Madonna/whore, the femme fatale and the beauty queen. Cogan plays with feminine sexuality and perspective, allegorical and abject in her narrative.

~~~~~ Cogan takes up the narrative of the fabric's past life in her found 'canvases', taking the existing hand-embroidery on the old table runners, bureau scarves and tablecloths as conventions she can embellish to subvert. Flower motifs embedded in the cloth float around her stitched figures in a Gauguin Tahiti-like breeze as they embellish bodies but do nothing to cover up the intimate parts and gestures those bodies express. They seem to suggest a flux between the women's assertive and passive roles as they embrace and ignore each other with each passing fancy.

~~~~~ Red nails and red nipples compliment green leaves and twinning vines in a twist of postmodern perversity alluding to old and new anxieties, insecurities, vanities and desires. The fabric becomes the canvas on which Cogan weaves an exotic dialogue of dichotomies. The tactile and nurturing association of the hand-stitched 'women's work' is turned into something evocative and unexpected with the embellished pubic hair perfectly entwined with the colourful narrative of the moment.

Orly Cogan, *Sweet Obsessions*, 2007.
Hand-stitched embroidery, applique and paint on fabric, 121.9 x 121.9 cm.

~~~~~ Cogan's photographic work includes red stitching into real flowers in situ, drawing environmental reference to her twisting vines and leafy details made fantastic by touches of artificial red. The male/female dynamic and paradisiacal framing are suggestive of the Adam and Eve scenario, and symbols of fertility and the cycle of life are strewn throughout her scenes with superficial, often seemingly random placing. Everything from punnets of strawberries to clowns and men with pantomime sheep heads float around the work in what feels like a childlike application. Some pieces appear to explore circus themes while others are touching tributes to close relations, as expressed in *Tangledupinyou* and *Wonder of You*. Cogan also directly explores issues around female identity and vice, sometimes choosing to depict themes of binge eating or drug abuse.

~~~~~ Within the majority of her work, Cogan evidences a desire to create a thought-provoking narrative investigating the changing nature of the female in contemporary society. What role do women want to play? Who do women want to be? What kind of relationships do women want to share? Who is the modern female role model? Her works illustrates the shifting boundaries within contemporary human culture, particularly those that define our relationships and, indeed, ourselves.

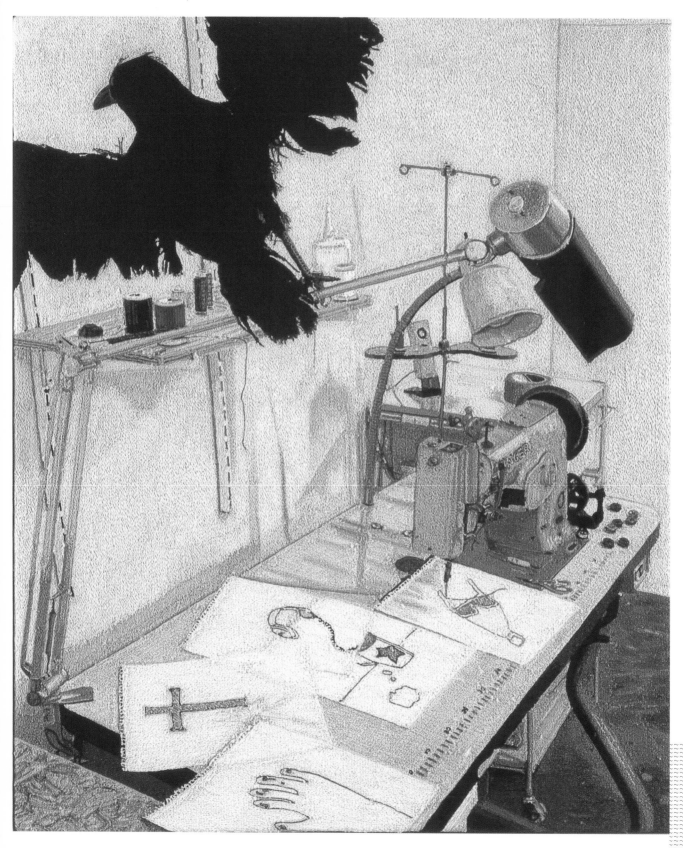

Satoru Aoyama, *Crowing in the Studio: Overview*, 2007.
Embroidery on polyester, 40.8 x 34.6 cm. Image courtesy of the artist and Mizuma Art Gallery. Photo: Kei Miyajima.

Satoru Aoyama, *Crowing in the Studio: Paint and Brush*, 2007.
Embroidery on polyester, 34.3 x 41.5cm. Image courtesy of the artist and Mizuma Art Gallery. Photo: Keizo Kioku.

Satoru Aoyama

Satoru Aoyama uses embroidery to produce a series of pictorial compositions ranging from mundane, everyday objects and scenes—a bunch of roses, a gold chain, a lighted candle, a sewing machine—to portraits, cityscapes and landscapes. Though the subject matter often varies from piece to piece, the process remains consistent throughout his work. Aoyama uses his own photographs, which he traces into paper or fabric as his starting point. After draft upon draft, he gradually builds up an image ready for development, which he then embroiders using an old industrial sewing machine. His method is painstaking: intricate layers of colour stitches and subtle gradations of texture and tone make up each of his works, meticulously executed to produce startlingly convincing scenes. Aoyama's photographs are transformed, through delicate and laborious craftsmanship, into something like a completely new discipline or form, utterly changing the nature and meaning of the photographic original.

~~~~~ These works are so complex in their construction that, from a distance, they appear to be carefully-worked drawings, posing an interesting question as to the continued relevance of the art/craft divide in contemporary art. Aoyama bridges the gap between the fine and decorative arts, between the ornamental and the conceptual, encapsulating one of the mostly hotly contested debates in textile art.

Bente Sœtrang, ...*day after day 7*, 2007.
Computer modified photograph printed on fine fiberpaper, part of *Textile and Tragedy* series, 2006–2007, 43 x 43 cm.

Fembarnsmoren Mariam Shihabiyah er én av mange Beirut-boere som har mistet det meste

' **kuddlinjen.** I går forlot over 200 nordmenn Beirut med bus

Bente Sœtrang

Trained in art textiles, Norwegian-born Bente Sœtrang is one of the pioneers of fabric printing in her home country, but has also made waves with her textile-inspired artworks on the international stage. Her recent work focuses on how humans have aspired to make their surroundings, and themselves, beautiful and meaningful through the use of textiles, whether through the objects placed in the home or the clothing worn on the body.

~~~~~ Sœtrang once worked exclusively in the realm of fabric printing, but she has since moved towards pencil and paper work. However her methods have evolved, the theme of textiles has remained a focus throughout her creative practice, now choosing to depict beautifully rendered, often jarring, scenes in graphite that portray the use of textiles by various individuals in different settings. Fabric objects are

taken out of their familiar domestic settings and placed in an unlikely context, alongside an animated human subject, or subjects. In these fine pencil drawings, Sœtrang will often construct the bulk of the image as a graphite and paper stage, upon which she enlivens the textile object depicted with lavish additions of colour. By removing the textile objects from the settings we expect to find them in, they bear no relationship to anything other than the individual they are pictured with, thereby strengthening the bond between person and fabric in a manner that can often be melancholic, confusing or disturbing.

Tucker Schwarz, *Just you wait*, 2006
Drawing, Thread on muslin, 41.9cm x 58.4cm, Photo: John White

Tucker Schwarz

Tucker Schwarz uses a sewing machine to render intricately detailed 'drawings' in thread on muslin, creating delicate scenes derived from personal memories or photographs taken of residential neighbourhoods.

~~~~~ The pieces range in scale from postcard to bedsheet-size, depicting lonely street corners and quiet suburban facades. The representations evidence the technical accuracy of the architectural draftsman, but the effect of the scant lines on neutral backgrounds, and the loose, wispy ends of the thread creates a sense of unease. What one critic labelled Schwarz' "rhetoric of crisis" begins to communicate the "ever-nagging implication that things are about to fall apart". Her complex psychogeography evokes suburban alienation and an atmosphere of fragility.

~~~~~ Schwarz' more recent three-dimensional installations, or "networks", develop this suggestion of things being "loosely held together". The threads are suspended in space rather than on a canvas, resembling spider webs, "illustrations of our inter-dependence". These works evoke the notion of a necessary togetherness, one in which one thread's undoing would cause the entire structure to collapse. However understated, Schwarz' work is quietly poignant, speaking volumes about the anxieties of the modern urban experience.

1. Olsen, Marisa, "Tucker Schwarz at Gregory Lind Gallery", *Artweek*, June 2005.
2. Taken from the artist's statement, submitted to the author in November 2007.

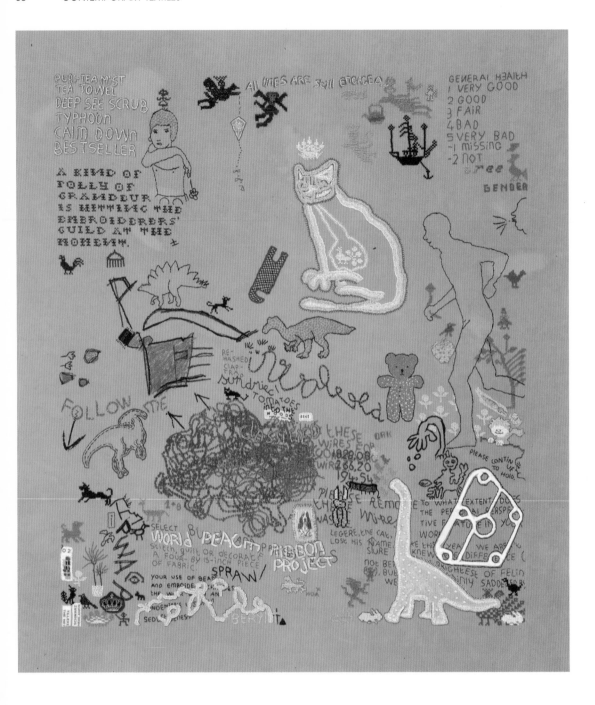

OPPOSITE: Tilleke Schwarz, *Welcome to the real world*, 2001.
Hand-embroidery and stitching on linen, cotton and silk yarns on linen, 66 x 68 cm.

Tilleke Schwarz, *Into the Woods*, 2002.
Hand-embroidery, silk, cotton and rayon yarn on dyed linen cloth, pieces of material, lace and textile paint, 66 x 74 cm.

Tilleke Schwarz

Dutch artist Tilleke Schwarz uses techniques such as cross-stitching and couching to produce delicate embroideries with a contemporary twist. Schwarz embroiders all of her dyed linen samplers by hand; a time-consuming process that may take months to yield one finished piece.

~~~~~ Schwarz was classically trained as a fine artist at the Free Academy for Modern Art in The Hague, but her work has rich affinities with non-institutionalised creative practices: childlike, oneiric and whimsical, her embroidered collages are reminiscent of the some of the best folk, street or outsider art. Her work resonates with unusual imagery, graffiti-like texts, and startling juxtapositions. CoBrA, a post-Second World War artistic movement that played a crucial role in the development of modern and contemporary art in The Netherlands, emerges as an obvious

influence. Lack of a preconceived plan, an intuitive, spontaneous approach to art-making, a fascination with primitive art, handwriting, mythology and folklore and a preoccupation with animals and mythical or prehistoric beings are themes taken up in both Schwarz and the CoBrA group´s work. "We used everything and loved everything" Corneille, a founding CoBrA member once said "We took from children´s drawings, folklore, drawings by the insane, negro masks…"[1]. Similarly Schwarz draws inspiration from a multitude of sources, from traditional samplers, to literary texts and objects she encounters in her everyday life. Her meticulous cut-and-paste methodology results in abstract, loosely-defined compositions that are often fantastical or unusual, while simultaneously maintaining strong ties to reality. Works such as *Into the Woods* or the aptly titled *Welcome to the Real World*

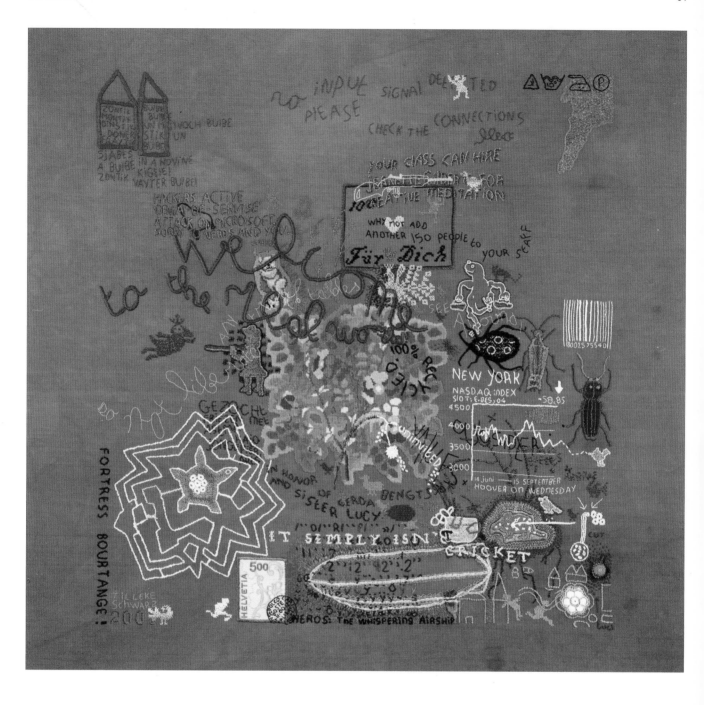

contain references to topical, everyday life—from the latest breakthroughs in contemporary textile practice to American presidential elections and letters written to the editor of the Embroiderers Guild. Her work thus oscillates between fantasy and reality, dream and waking life, the personal and the political.

Schwarz' juxtapositions emphasise free association, processes and narratives of disjointedness. In the tradition of the Modernist novel, her work contains narrative elements that remain open-ended, unresolved and ambiguous, with neither ends nor beginnings. "On the contrary" she explains "the narrative structures are used as a form of communication with the viewer. The viewer is invited to decipher connections or to create them".[2]

1. From the CoBrA Museum website, http://www.cobra-museum.nl/en/cobra.html#TheCoBrAstyle, retrieved 1 February 2008.
2. From the artist's statement, submitted to the author in August 2007.

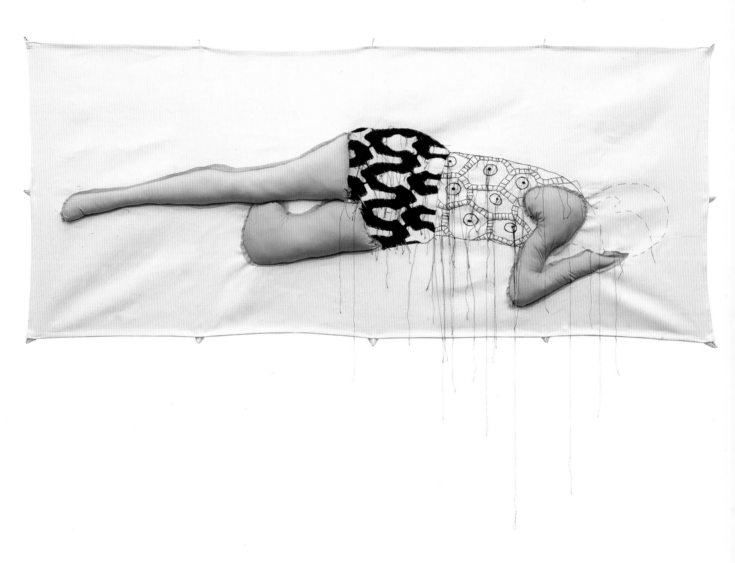

Sybille Hotz

Sybille Hotz takes her first point of reference from medical textbooks and technical manuals, culling inspiration from schematic illustrations depicting the human body during illness or injury, technical representations of organs or simply the interior of the human form in a general sense. Hotz uses these images as raw material from which to devise her soft sculptures, or design patterns to be repeated as abstract embellishment. She often uses the form and shape of organs as an ornamental subject with which to decorate the exterior of the body, literally turning the human form inside out, exposing the materiality of the human essence, its frailty and flexibility. At times surprisingly explicit, Hotz' work is never gory or macabre, but rather often expressed in a celebratory or playful spirit.

~~~~~ The metaphor of textile as skin courses through Hotz' work, employing unfinished, undyed fabrics as vessels for her sculptural forms, upon which she embroiders patterns suggestive of an interior that will not be contained. She often leaves loose threads hanging from her work, emphasising an incompleteness and unrealised potential in the structures themselves. This element of the incomplete is expressed through Hotz' choice of subject, often depicting unresolved narrative scenes that compel the viewer to probe further, imagining the last act in the drama being played out before them. Hotz uses untreated natural materials because they possess a familiarity that instantly creates an emotional closeness with the works themselves, situating the viewer within a recognisable physical world where various surprising connotations and meanings can be brought into play.

PAIN

TINGS

Steve Mac Donald, *Untitled*.
Embroidered painting, thread, canvas, acrylic paint, 106.68 cm ft x 152.4 cm. Image courtesy of the artist.

Steve MacDonald

San Francisco-based artist Steve MacDonald creates embroidered paintings on gilded canvases. His work draws inspiration from an eclectic array of sources including Japanese nature scenes, folk art, fantasy, mythology and elements from the urban experience. Taken together, his compositions provoke a variety of spontaneous references through the depiction of fantastical landscapes. A variety of imagery act out fantastical narratives, where tigers, rainbows, cityscapes, skulls and shipping containers are juxtaposed against the backdrop of a traditional Japanese print form.

~~~~~ This merging of futuristic subject matter and historical setting underlines the mythical nature of MacDonald's creative method, preventing the viewer from getting too comfortable in one context or another and, rather, encouraging a more associative approach to understanding the work. The mood and pace of the stitching varies considerably from one painting to the next, often within a single work, using a different material language to describe the texture and lines of any given element, whether it be foliage, water, the peaks of a mountain range or the facade of a building.

~~~~~ There is something unpredictable, nearly magical, about these works, as if they would change form and character even between views. It is this fundamental spontaneity that makes MacDonald's work so engaging, drawing the viewer ever closer to the fantasy world of the canvas.

Berend Strik, *Curators Memory Aid*, 2006. C-print with embroidery, 89 x 82 cm. Image courtesy Galerie Fons Welters, Amsterdam. Photo: Arjan Bennink.

Berend Strik

Dutch artist Berend Strik has been working in different disciplines over the past 20 years: from sculpture, to architectural collaborations, to two-dimensional works. Not tied to any particular medium, Strik describes his practice as belonging to the loosely defined sphere of post-disciplinary visual art.

~~~~~ Strik brings the sensibility of a painter to the medium of embroidery: seen from a distance his works often give the impression of painterly compositions. In truth these are photographs he has appropriated from a variety of sources—personal or family archives, books, magazines, or images he encounters in his travels. The original photograph is sometimes reproduced in its entirety, and sometimes combined with other images to form embroidered collages. Images are often blurred or out of focus and stitched with delicate threads that render them abstract and ambiguous. In his earlier embroideries, Strik used photographs of a rather explicit nature, but nowadays his imagery is more subtle: tranquil landscapes, architectural scenes and childhood photographs replace the hardcore pornographic material of his late 1980s work. Likewise his embroidery has oscillated between extreme interventions of needlework that alter the original to the point of obliteration and minimal stitches that faithfully reproduce the photographic original.

~~~~~ Strik's work tackles themes characteristic of much post-Second World War artistic practice. He questions painting's claims to originality and artistic grandeur by choosing a medium that is often relegated to the realm of the decorative. Yet painting looms large within his practice and Strik undermines the reproducibility of the original photograph by giving it a more autonomous, painterly, form.

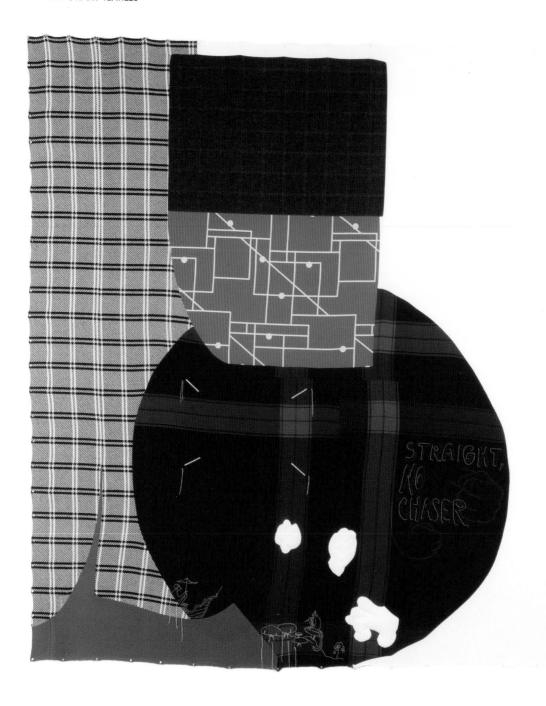

OPPOSITE: Cosima von Bonin, *DEPRIONEN, A VOYAGE TO THE SEA*, 2006.
Cotton, linen, 319 x 357 cm.

Cosima von Bonin, *STRAIGHT, NO CHASER*, 2007.
Mixed media, 310 x 265 cm.

Cosima von Bonin

One of the most influential and prolific artists working in Germany today, Cosima von Bonin has maintained a diverse artistic practice since the early 1990s, one that has combined sculpture, performance, music, film, video and textile paintings. An important principle informing Von Bonin's work is the contrasted use of colours, shapes and materials, and the transformation of common forms into oversized sculptures, from the giant mushrooms that kept reappearing in her early installations to the larger-than-life stuffed animals of her 2007 solo exhibition at the Museum of Contemporary Art in Los Angeles. Her work has touched upon themes of discipline and indoctrination, failure and success, role-playing and gender representations.
~~~~~ Difficult to categorise, the Cologne-based artist has moved through different roles (curator, artist, producer, historian) and has consciously created

work that lacks a coherent, homogeneous style. This might be why, as Yilmaz Dziewior argues, von Bonin seems like a perpetually potential artist, one lacking a clear-cut, finite set of concerns.[1] The artist's essential lack of definition may be in part due to her commitment to the principles of collaboration, and the fluidity of the creative method.
~~~~~ In the past decade, Von Bonin has often used textiles such as wool, felt, printed fabrics and loden cloth to make costumes for performances, upholstery for her sculptural installations and what she calls her *Lappen* (rags), a series of fabric collage works that incorporate ready-made textiles and found imagery. The rags recall both Mike Kelley's banners and Sigmar Polke's work, combining swaths of fabric with text, embroidered or cut out figures and other material to

affect a bold painterly style. Von Bonin's work challenges the limits of the Modernist programme, taking up themes of 'women's work' and conventional perceptions of feminine activity.

~~~~~ Von Bonin's artistic practice privileges the social, the immediate, and resonates with a utopian belief in collaboration that is reminiscent of the early European Avant-Garde, with its calculated tactics for subverting the cult of the individual artist through ideas of friendship, influence and apprenticeship. She sometimes uses her own exhibitions as a platform for the presentation of her friend's work. Indeed in her 1991 exhibition at Andrea Kosen gallery in New York, von Bonin turned a purportedly solo exhibition into a group show, including work by fellow artists Martin Kippenberger, Mayo Thompson, Isabelle Graw and Jutta Koether. This belief in collaboration is consistent throughout von Bonin's practice; even her solo work resonates with a multitude of references to other artists—Bas Jan Ader, Marcel Broodthaers, Poul Gernes—to name a few. The open-endedness of her approach challenges orthodox views about ownership, artistic identity and authorship, and rather expresses creative method as something essentially discursive and performative.

1. Dziewior, Yilmaz, "Wag the Dog", *Artforum,* November 2007.

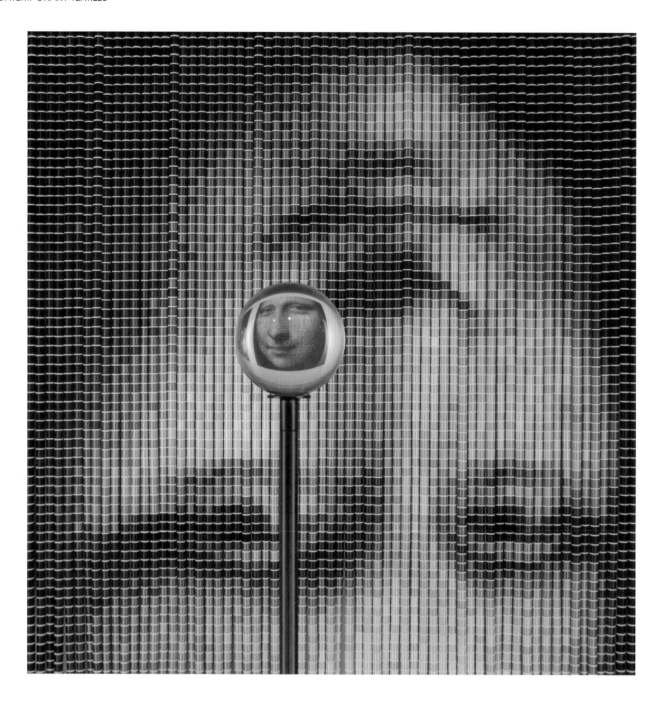

OPPOSITE: Devorah Sperber, *After The Last Supper*, 2005.
Thread Spools, 274.3 x 2213.36 x 883.92 cm.

Devorah Sperber, *After The Mona Lisa 2*, 2005.
Thread Spools, dimensions unavailable.

Devorah Sperber

At the heart of Devorah Sperber's practice is the experience of viewing art in the context of technically reproduced and manipulated images, which come to be described in works that challenge our understanding of the visual, and indeed of perception itself. Originally a stone carver, by the end of the 1990s Sperber had begun to seek out ways of incorporating her fascination with digital imagery with the sculptural methods familiar to her. From this investigation the artist developed her, now characteristic, method of constructing 'pixelated' image-objects. To view Sperber's work is to become involved in a strange temporal interplay, in which paintings by Old Masters are made using contemporary technologies, and the long-familiar and recognisable collides with the unforeseen in new and provocative ways.

~~~~~ In *After The Last Supper* and *After the Mona Lisa 2*, thousands of spools of coloured thread hang in a grid, forming great chromatic scenes that may be viewed as abstract assemblages in their own right. However, when viewed through a small acrylic sphere, these three-dimensional constructions are suddenly and unexpectedly amalgamated into clear, recognisable likenesses of the works cited in Sperber's titles. Here, the historical use of visual aids (*camera obscura*) and Sperber's 'magical' crystal ball display are played off ideas of authenticity, appropriation and the virtual. At the level of what Sperber calls "intellectual concepts", she regards these works as incorporating the science of vision into the creative method—such as the ability, or inability, of the brain to take incomplete visual information and form a cohesive whole through cognitive and intellectual mechanisms.

~~~~~ Given her conceptual drives, it is not surprising that, in 2003, Sperber developed a series of works involving incrementally different 'resolutions', based on the subject of cyberneticist Leon Harmon's 1973 study *The Recognition of Faces*. Harmon investigated human perception by creating a pixelated image of Abraham Lincoln to test the thresholds of facial recognition, famously inspiring Salvador Dali's painting *Gala Contemplating the Mediterranean Sea*. It is this Dali piece that Sperber took as the subject of her *After Dali, After Harmon*, constructed from thousands of coloured chenille pipe cleaners fixed into foam board. Indeed, in many of the paintings, Sperber recreates the method involved in creating the original she reproduces, in the case, a consideration of the parameters of visual recognition, a thread picked up not only in the visual ambiguities of her assemblages

but in the convex mirrors, transparent viewing spheres and reflective steel surfaces she installs to allow the viewer multiple points of entry to the work. It is in this way—layering multiple references and visual components—that Sperber's works become so totally engaging. As such these pieces prompt a re-examination of the parameters by which objects are recognised as real or discreet, revealing the physical and subjective mechanisms by which we understand the visual world around us, and thereby opening that world to the potential of interpretation.

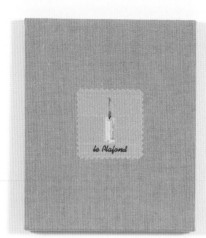

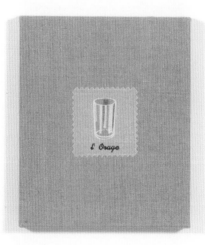

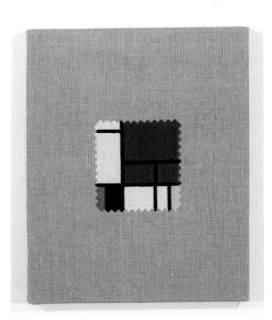

Elaine Reichek, *Swatches, Mondrian 1–4*, 2007.
Digital embroidery on linen, Overall dimensions: 67.3 x 57.2 cm, each panel: 30.5 x 25.4 cm, edition of three.

OPPOSITE: Elaine Reichek, *Swatches, Magritte 1-9* 2007.
Digital embroidery on linen, overall dimensions: 104.1 x 88.9 cm, each panel: 30.5 x 25.4 cm, edition of three.

Elaine Reichek

Elaine Reichek is one of the first conceptual artists to use knitting and embroidery as a means of subverting accepted ideas about originality, authenticity and the myth of the artistic genius. Since the late 1970s she has produced a diverse and complex body of work that explores the dynamics of power, identity, sexuality and representation.

~~~~~ Reichek trained as an artist under the guidance of Ad Reinhardt, a painter, writer and pioneer of conceptual and minimal art who had a great impact on her work. However, she soon adopted a critical stance to her training and in 1978 began to show work in non-traditional media such as collage, photography, knitting and installation, with embroidery gradually becoming the focus of her artistic practice.

~~~~~ It is perhaps easy to underestimate the radical nature of Reichek's choice, now that craft has been further integrated into the contemporary art establishment,

but, in the late 1970s, needlework was still confined to the realms of the decorative and the domestic. Reichek's mistrust of both canonical art history and the tenants of the Modernist rhetoric necessitated an approach and a choice of medium that posed a challenge to patriarchal art and its tools—brush, paint, canvas—by substituting them with media usually perceived as feminine. Along with her contemporaries, Judy Chicago and Kate Walker, Reichek would thus operate within traditionally feminine methodologies in order to communicate difficult and challenging ideas about womanhood, gender and sexuality.

~~~~~ Her primary source of inspiration has been the sampler of the eighteenth and nineteenth centuries—a piece of embroidery produced as a demonstration of technical expertise in needlework—where flowers, trees and animals were

arranged to produce a geometrically-balanced picture, often featuring religious or moral inscriptions. Reichek has produced beautiful samplers making use of traditional motifs and geometrical designs in repeating border patterns, while simultaneously introducing entirely untraditional information. She substitutes the typical moral or religious inscriptions with quotes from sources as diverse as art history, architecture, literature, philosophy, science, mythology and popular culture.

~~~~ In *Sampler (Starting Over)*, she embroiders a quote from Homer in which Penelope describes her secret un-weaving of the work she has done during the day: "I wound my schemes on my distaff—I would weave that mighty web by day— But then by night, by torchlight—I undid what I had done". This, she juxtaposes with a quote from her teacher Reinhardt: "Starting over at the beginning, always

the same—perfection of beginnings, eternal return—creation, destruction, eternal repetition—made, unmade, remade." There are powerful analogies to be drawn here, as for Reichek, art-making is clearly a process of continuous creation, destruction and revision.

~~~~ Among her other sources, Reichek counts references to Arachne, a mythical creature who discovered the use of linen and nets, and was transformed into a spider by the goddess Athena, and the Three Fates, the triple spinning goddesses who weaved the thread of life and destiny. In other work, quotes from literature are abundant: extracts from Charlotte Bronte's *Shirley* ("She was knitting in the alcove—her task of work on her knee, her fingers assiduously plying the needle, continuously, easelessly, but her brain worked faster than her fingers."), Charles

Elaine Reichek, *Sampler (Troilus and Cressida)*, 2001. Embroidery on linen, 67.9 x 46.7 cm.

OPPOSITE: Elaine Reichek, *Sampler (Moby Dick)*, 1997. Embroidery on linen, 44.5 x 34.3 cm.

Troilus and Cressida

Women are angels, wooing:
Things won are done, joy's soul lies in the doing.
That she belov'd knows nought that knows not this:
Men prize the thing ungain'd more than it is.
That she was never yet that ever knew
Love got so sweet as when desire did sue.
Therefore this maxim out of love I teach:
Achievement is command; ungain'd, beseech.

— William Shakespeare

Elaine Reichek

Dickens' *A Tale of Two Cities* ("darkness closed around. So much was closing in about the women who sat knitting, knitting… knitting, knitting, counting dropping heads.") and Henry James' *The Art of Fiction* ("Experience is never limited, and it is never complete, it is an immense sensibility, a kind of huge spider-web of the finest silken threads suspended.") fill the frames of her embroidered samplers, adding a conceptual weight to a medium that has been traditionally relegated to the status of craft.

Quotation and cultural appropriation are indeed the hallmarks of Reichek's work. For her latest exhibition at the Nicole Klagsbrun Gallery, *Pattern Recognition*, the artist replicated paintings by modern and contemporary artists through the use of a computer-programmed sewing machine. Artworks by René Magritte,

Piet Mondrian, Henri Matisse, Philip Guston, Andy Warhol, Damien Hirst and Nancy Spero were digitally embroidered in small fabric swatches—long used in the textile industry. These tiny needlepoint replicas convey a multiplicity of meanings and messages and resonate with the contradictions and paradoxes ever-present in Reichek's oeuvre: high versus low, originality versus repetition, tradition versus technology.

OPPOSITE: Ghada Amer, *White drips on white*, 2003. Embroidery and acrylic on canvas, 183 x 214 cm. Image courtesy of Galleria Massimo Minini.

Ghada Amer, *A Missed Kiss*, 2002. Embroidery and acrylic on canvas, 183 x 163 cm. Image courtesy of Galleria Massimo Minini.

Ghada Amer

Ghada Amer was born in Cairo in 1963, and grew up in the politically-charged atmosphere following the events of the Six-Day War. In 1974 she relocated to France to begin her artistic training, graduating in 1989 and later moving to New York where she currently lives and works. She has exhibited at the Venice Biennale, and is the first Arab artist to have a one-person exhibition at the Tel Aviv Museum of Art. For over a decade, Amer has addressed fundamental dichotomies of east versus west, fine art versus craft, and the feminine versus the masculine through her sculptures, public garden projects, paintings and embroideries.

~~~~~ Amer's relocations had a profound impact upon her artistic practice, with the continuous shifting of meanings and the hybridisation of identities operating as the guiding conceptual principles behind her work. Amer constantly situates herself in a position of the relative, simultaneously within and outside conflicting cultures, identities, philosophies and civilisations. Her work has been characterised as feminist, Muslim, French and Abstract-Expressionist, to name just a few terms, but the artist has frequently protested against the trappings of—often all too easy—definitions and categories. Her work is at once everything and none of the above, a rich, complex and eclectic amalgam of disparate elements that shatters the illusions of national, aesthetic and cultural purity while remaining forever elusive.

~~~~~ It is no wonder that the subject of religious and moral fundamentalism is one to which we find Amer returning again and again: Amer takes issue with the narrow perspective promulgated by the Islamic authorities in works such as

Private Room, 2000, where selected quotes form the Qu'ran dealing with women ("A slave who believes is more valuable than a free and polytheistic woman" reads one of them) are embroidered in long rows of coloured hanging satin. Amer's expression of dismay at the oppressive laws governing womens' attitudes towards their own bodies has been consistent throughout her work, bolstered by the artist's own experience while travelling in her native country.

~~~~~ Amer does indeed appropriate feminist tactics, but refuses to adhere to feminism's more radical strands. For Amer, feminism is a possible tool among many: the moment when subversive philosophies become encompassing, rigid and life-denying systems of thought is an uneasy one for the artist. If first-wave feminist thought sought to prevent the physical and intellectual victimisation of women through a denial of the body, Amer's subtle yet profound work revels in an unapologetic celebration of female sexuality. "I believe that all women" she claims "should like their bodies and use them as tools of seduction". In her well-known erotic embroideries, Amer copies pornographic images of women from commercial erotica—of the sort typically demonised by feminist criticism—and reclaims them for her own use. By outlining explicit sexual acts in needle and thread she also infuses them with a tenderness and delicacy absent from their original context.

~~~~~ Similarly her attitude towards her Islamic heritage resonates with ambivalence. Named after a Medieval Islamic compilation of texts dealing with human sexuality, her *Encyclopedia of Pleasure* is both a telling metaphor on the

Ghada Amer

repression of female sexuality in Islam and a gesture of love towards the artist's native culture. Amer challenges monolithic conceptions of the middle east by reminding the viewer of some of the more radical elements of non-institutionalised Islam, while simultaneously offering a powerful treatise on censorship and the repression of sexuality (the compilation has been banned in Islam since the seventeenth century).

~~~~~ Her 2007 installation, *Le Salon Courbé,* at Fransesca Minini gallery in Milan evidences the artist's continued engagement with the issue of fundamentalism, but this time from a post-9/11 perspective. Amer sets ups the gallery space as a lounge where visual elements of both western and middle eastern cultures co-exist in an ambiguous and politically-charged *mise-en-scène.* Egyptian carpets and neo-colonialist-style furniture are situated within vibrantly coloured walls, decorated in patterned wallpaper that evokes both the western and Arabic tradition. There is an alarming tension lurking beneath the seemingly welcoming *décor,* as the viewer is confronted with complex definitions of the English word for terrorism that date back to the French Revolution and the Reign of Terror. These are embedded in the wallpaper and elaborated in adjacent canvases where definitions of words such as love, peace, security and freedom are embroidered in Arabic, underlining the lack of a coherent definition for terrorism in the Arabic language. *Le Salon* attempts to dissociate the identification of Muslim with violence, a link sadly prevalent in media representations of our time, and rather raises complex—at times uncomfortable—questions about the

Ghada Amer, *Le Salon Courbé*, 2007.
Embroidery, fabric, wallpaper, wood, dimensions variable. Image courtesy of Francesca Minini.

role of the west in determining moral categories on the international stage. What if, Amer seems to hint, terrorism is a specifically western construct whose very definition is highly contestable?

~~~~~ Amer's work succeeds at regenerating a sense of critical attention to the ethical and political complexity of our time. Amidst an international drive for absolute definitions of good and evil, Amer's courage and conceptual rigour cuts a fine swathe through the rhetoric and spin characteristic of the War on Terror. She allows her practice to be guided by startling tensions and conflicting meanings and counters the languages of closure and enmity through unresolved narratives of hope, longing and love.

LEFT: Gillian Cooper, *Vigilance VIII*.
Wall hanging, Felted knitted textile, 70 x 140 cm.

RIGHT: Gillian Cooper, *Vigilance IX*,
Wall hanging, Felted knitted textile, 70 x 140 cm.

Gillian Cooper

"Paint on its own seems sterile by comparison."

~~~~~ Gillian Cooper works predominantly in knit, constructing intricate forms which express her understanding of a world presented through the media, incorporating the themes of protection, safety and urban anxiety. Cooper uses CCTV stills, which she reworks as felted hangings that evoke an eerie, ominous and ambiguous quality. Our usual experience of CCTV imagery is in the aftermath of crime—a grainy series of stills, presented as a jerky, awkward stop-animation, usually depicting a victim's final moments or a crime in progress. Cooper utilises the visual quality of CCTV as cultural signifier to create a sense of danger or suspense, heightening the awareness of the viewer to the narrative of the image depicted. Cooper taps into our collective anxiety in an unlikely guise, using

elements of the fabric medium—"reminiscent of blankets, which are a very basic form of protection from the cold"—and juxtaposing them against the stark, nearly monotonal, schemes of the work.

~~~~~ Despite embracing textile as a medium, Cooper is aware of her misgivings as a seamstress, "I can't sew in the traditional sense and wouldn't know how to make curtain, which is what most people seem to assume a textile degree trains you to do". Cooper is firmly situated in her artistic product rather than the process of its creation and unlike many other textile artists, focuses attention on the concepts underlining the work rather than the mechanics of production.

Monica Auch, *Immigrants 2*.
Wall panel, Silk, light reflective yarns, organza, 45 x 30 cm.

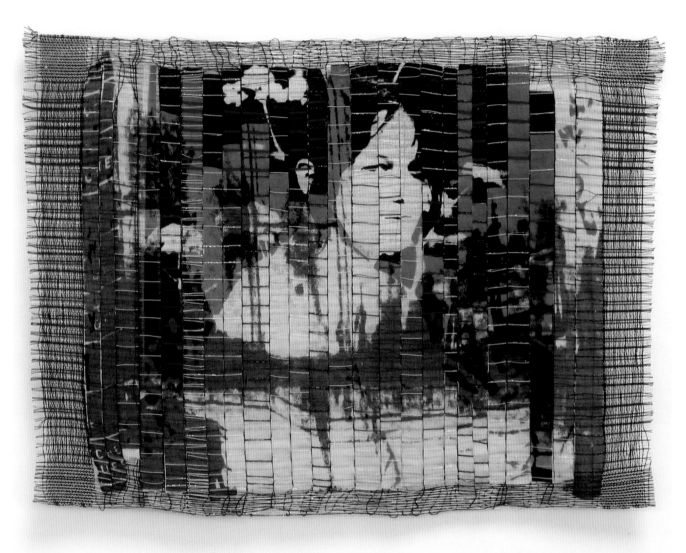

Monika Auch

Monica Auch's medical background is evident in her detailed textile work, which is often suggestive of the growth patterns found through the lens of a microscope. The work feels both startlingly real and somehow fragmented, expressing the bare amounts of detail required for the viewer to recognise forms and narratives. The clash of digital and tactile methods in Auch's work heightens the material impact of the viewing experience, a combination of traditional, time-consuming methods and contemporary, instantaneous technology.

~~~~~ For Auch, the worlds of art and medicine are inextricably bound together with both professions requiring the same core skills: a knack of understanding humans and their environment, heightened haptic senses and well-developed spatial orientation. "After six years of art practice, a symbiosis between these skills has grown , I am a true hybrid—a mixture of science and art."[1] Auch makes no distinction between the various forms of her creative expression. The success of her work appears to stem from this unlikely pairing of interests— as Auch states, "I do not think that art, intuition and science are separate ways of thinking".[2] More than that, her unique viewpoint lends her work a refreshingly original perspective, one that is as dramatic as it is detailed, approaching a variety of themes from multiple perspectives and areas of human enquiry.

1. Taken from the artist's statement, submitted to the author in November 2007.
2. Taken from the artist's statement, submitted to the author in November 2007.

Janis Jefferies, *Green Source Code*.
Rayon, 150 x 70 cm. Photo: David Ramkalawon.

Janis Jefferies

As an artist, curator and writer, Janis Jefferies has contributed extensively to the practice and theory of textile art over the past 25 years. Her work involves the translation of digital information into dynamic fabrics, either printed or Jacquard woven. Her reputation has grown with exhibitions in Britain, Poland, America, Canada and Australia, and with numerous conferences and professorships across the globe. She currently holds the positions of Professor of Visual Arts, Artistic Director of Goldsmiths Digital Studios at Goldsmiths College, and Director of the Constance Howard Resource and Research Centre in Textiles.

~~~~~ Her early work haunts and disturbs the viewer; unpopulated spaces are lit from high windows, unmade beds and laundry bundles whisper about past occupants, narrative scraps and anecdotes of lost lives. They grope at ephemeral meanings, histories and possible futures, while holding residual references to objects and material forms that ask the audience to participate in the mortality and fragility of another. Silence, ultimately, is heard loudest as the images contend with the absence and suspension of the world of the living. "I am now my own spectator. Although tantalisingly held at a distance I move closer to these images... scraps, anecdotes of lost lives. One might even find a temporary repose in lingering with an image or set of images as the site of the residue of objects, of material, and in the recognition that to take an image is to participate in another's mortality, vulnerability, mutability. Life is suspended, sudden death created. Sometimes the silence of the image is so great it disturbs."[1] Jefferies movingly captures the very essence of longing, and the grey nostalgia of great emotional loss.

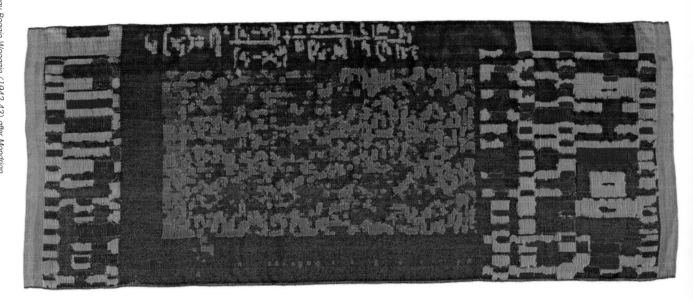

Janis Jefferies, *Ave Maria*, 2005, *meets Broadway Boogie Wooggie (1942-43) after Mondrian.*
Jacquard, Rayon, 150 x 70 cm. Photo: David Ramkalawon.

~~~~ Her latest work, *A Sound you can Touch,* in conjunction with Dr Tim Blackwell, explores the relationship between sound and visual experience in performance pieces. Jefferies maps textile images, taken from scans of complex weaving patterns generated by the Jacquard loom, into aural structures that can be played to an audience, offering a totally new point of entry into the world of textiles. The resulting work incorporates the most cutting edge digital technology to transform the virtual warp and weft of mutating textile patterns into sonic improvisation, creating an environmental installation where the immediate haptic and abstract aural qualities of the material are made available for a multi-sensorial experience. Jefferies' method is based on a complex 'Swarm' abstraction animation process that unpacks the fascinating micro-texture of virtual surfaces, investigating the space in between accessible dimensions of material objects where alternate worlds of experience might reside.

~~~~ The work probes notions of creativity and glimpses into possible meanings and connections between mobile bodies of sound and image and texture in time and space. A pioneer of textile art, Jefferies continues to push the boundaries of multi-disciplinary artistic practice, forever embracing new technologies and techniques in her unstinting quest for new expressions and forms.

1. The artist quoted in: Leong, Greg, *JAB,* Maitland Museum and Art Gallery NSW, Australia, December 2006.

Kent Henricksen

Kent Henricken's work is a humourous and surrealist take on the darker aspects of the human psyche. In his embroideries, he uses both *Toile de Jouy* found fabrics and textiles of his own design, which he creates by silk-screening images onto fabric. The patterns are iconographically inspired by the French Rococo of Boucher and Fragonard and depict scenes of a light-hearted picturesque world where couples fall in love, children dance about and cherubs float serenely through the air. There is a tremendous innocence conveyed by these works, strengthened by Henricksen's use of the traditional medium of embroidery and its connotations of domesticity, comfort and familiarity. Henricksen disrupts this superabundance by stitching menacing figures and scenes of physical violence. The beauty of the work is countered by narratives of submission, slavery and domination, in a Sadean environment where slaves become masters, children are disguised as executioners, and aristocrats are put to death.

~~~~~ Henricksen's embroideries reference a broad spectrum of historical themes, dealing with events that date back as far as the Reign of Terror and colonialism right through to current events. In works such as *Seduction* and *They Beat an Old Man*, hooded figures stand over the bodies of dead colonialists or dance with female children. Henricksen draws upon the rich connotations of the hood, a symbol that cuts through different cultures and historical periods, bearing tremendous associations, from medieval executioners, to present day terrorists.

~~~~~ Henricksen counts among his influences the black and white prints of the surrealist Max Ernst, in which the artist performed subtle yet bizarre alterations,

LEFT TO RIGHT: Kent Henricksen, Absence of Myth, 2007.
Silk-screen, embroidery thread and gold leaf on cotton, 116.8 x 142.2 cm.
Kent Henricksen, Marvelous Possessions, 2007.
Silk-screen, embroidery thread and gold leaf on silk, 116.8 x 127 cm.
Kent Henricksen, Burning Bedevilments, 2007.
Silk-screen, embroidery thread and gold leaf on silk, 116.8 x 149.9 cm.

the satirical engravings of Jose Guadalupe Posada and the apocalyptic paintings and woodcuts of Renaissance artist Albrecht Dürer. Art historical references co-exist with imagery drawn from old newspapers, historical volumes and magazine from the 1950s as well as texts borrowed from a variety of literary sources. Henricksen builds upon a wide-range of cross-cultural, cross-historical perspectives juxtaposing them and playing them against each other. His work is a kind of memory bank, a recollection of random past events combined into new and meaningful paradigms.

~~~~~ Henricksen delves beneath appearances to unsettle the false utopias of a collective denial of horrific acts being perpetrated in our own time and by our own cultures. His textiles enter into a dialogue with imagery suggestive of long and obscured histories of oppression. "I find the mixing" he explains "of the harsh, brutal sadism of human events with the intricate, decorative medium of embroidery is a way to riff on the reality in which we live, drawing attention to the passiveness that others feel for the atrocities in our world, when they are not directly theirs to deal with". Political, beautiful and unsettling, Henricksen's embroideries convey an uneasy mix of historical fact and fiction, exposing contradictions and tensions stricken from the official version of history.

OPPOSITE: Lara Schnitger, *Everybody Happy*, 2007.
Fabric on canvas, 157.5 x 198.1 cm. Image courtesy of Anton Kern Gallery, NY.

Lara Schnitger, *Untitled*, 2005.
Fabric, wood, 96.5 x 86.4 cm. Image courtesy of Anton Kern Gallery, NY.

Lara Schnitger

Lara Schnitger's work has developed over recent years to express themes of eroticism, politics, place and feminism within textiles-based creative method. Since the late 1990s, she has shifted away from her photographic and film work towards textile-based architectural installations. The themes is Schnitger's work have remained fundamentally consistent throughout her working life, with a focus on the female experience and themes of exploitation and eroticism expressing themselves through both her photographic and installation work.

~~~~~ Schnitger was heavily influenced by the legendary 1972 exhibition *Womanhouse*, curated by Miriam Schapiro and Judy Chicago. The show instigated a re-evaluation of traditional crafts stereotypically associated with women, such as knitting and pattern-making. It is this tradition that Schnitger takes up in her work, in a continued investigation into the efficacy of categories common to art criticism.

~~~~~ Her quirky brand of political commentary has become increasingly important to her work in recent years. 2005's *Grim Boy* and *Lost Hippie* play with cultural stereotypes with a fresh, often disturbing, tone. The amplified abstract mannequins explicitly confront the viewer with a visual encyclopaedia of prejudices alive in the popular imagination. More recently, Schnitger has used text as a core aspect of her work. By juxtaposing sexually charged prose with the innocuous quality of Womens' Institute-style crafts, the work has become more confrontational, conjuring up new meaning through the forced marriage of cross-cultural elements and a varied visual language.

~~~~~ Ideas of clashing cultures inform the political aspect of her work. For the 2005 *My Other Car is a Broom* exhibition Schnitger produced *Gridlock,* a piece constructed from bumper stickers referring to, amongst other things, the 2004 American presidential race between George Bush and John Kerry. The piece was inspired by her experience of Japanese construction sites and prayer flags from Tibet, exhibiting a fascination with layering impressions and experiences that runs right through her creative method. "In Japan, I saw Barbie Dolls and Hello Kitty next to old stone sculptures. I feel that our times are like that. This mixture of things makes perfect sense to me."[1] It is this interaction of various cultural and personal artefacts and symbols that drives much of Schnitger's creative practice, choosing to work in a multitude of visual and conceptual media.

~~~~~ Confrontation plays an increasingly important role in Schnitger's work. In *Piece of Shit,* she made the work difficult to navigate around to simultaneously intimidate and reward the spectator. It is these contrasting aspects within her work that make it so engaging: structure versus skin, the urban versus the rural, passive versus active, innocence versus vulgarity.

1. Taken from the artist's statement, submitted to the author in October 2007.

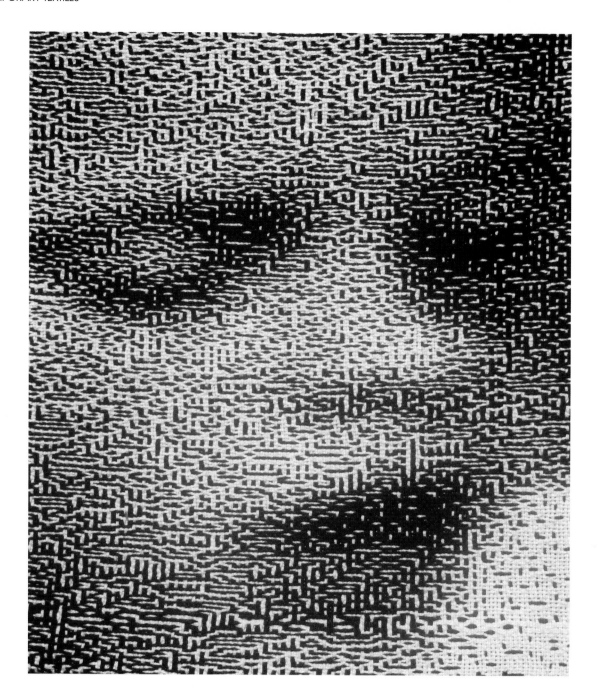

Lia Cook

Since the 1970s, Lia Cook has produced tapestries that explore the tactile and evocative qualities of cloth and its historical and personal connotations. Combining the manual techniques of weaving and painting with photography, film and a digital Jacquard loom, Cook's works investigate the ways in which a textile can be constructed through complex processes, and the attendant multiple possibilities of viewing, experiencing and understanding a piece.

~~~~~ In the 1990s, Cook developed a body of work taking drapery as both its subject and object. Traditionally a pictorial device of symbolic and framing purposes, Cook gave this long-established but often overlooked illustrative form new potency, transforming the ornamental into the monumental. The series *New Master Draperies* explored Renaissance representations of the subject, appropriating imagery from

Michaelangelo, Leonardo and Dürer and re-examining them through contemporary technologies and materials. Probing the transformative potential of textiles, her large-scale installation *Material Pleasures*, 1993, involved floor-length theatrical curtains themselves covered in representations of the folds of drapery which, in turn, framed six wall-mounted images, also of and on cloth. Mechanisms of representation are diffused and given fluctuating and alternate planes upon which to function: in looking, the threads that form Cook's images become loose and liquid, confounding our understanding of what is depicted and what is not, as embroidered images of folds are subsumed in swathes of fabric.

~~~~~ Other works also contain a human figure, as drapery wraps bodies in a shifting play of revealing and concealing: these pieces touch not only upon

Lia Cook, *Voices*, 2003. Textile, woven cotton, 188 x 139.7 cm. Image courtesy of the artist.

OPPOSITE: Lia Cook, *Four by Four*, 2007. Textile, woven cotton, 27.9 cm x 30.5 cm. Image courtesy of the artist.

our sensuous reception of memories and emotive experiences evoked through cloth but also explore the intricacies of the cloth-covered body. As the curtains in *Material Pleasures*, the textiles depicted obscure our view of the body and simultaneously, poignantly, enact a gesture of revealing that addresses both the instability of appearances and the tactile, sensual character of drapery.

It is this enquiry into the act of perceiving that weaves its way delicately through all of Cook's works. Recent pieces involving portraiture draw out the enigmatic and memorial qualities of photography and highlight the particular materiality of tapestry, so that the affective, emotive nature of the portrait collides with the detailed anatomy of woven cloth. Grainy and pixelated, these images shift constantly between the mysterious and the mundane: it is precisely the moment of oscillation between viewing a coherent image and being confronted close-up with fragmented, textural fabric that Cook is concerned with. The photo-realistic image, such as those that make up the *Traces* series, can be both banal and ethereal while similarly, the material facts of a tapestry's threads might appear simultaneously pedestrian and endlessly extraordinary. In Cook's Maze works, apparently coherent images can dissolve, through a shift in focus and virtually in the same instant, into labyrinthine constellations of marks and patterns, creating a jolt in the moment of recognition. Cook's work enables new discoveries and experiences within the act of viewing textile, by continually calling into question the representational qualities of cloth and drawing attention to the complexities of its construction.

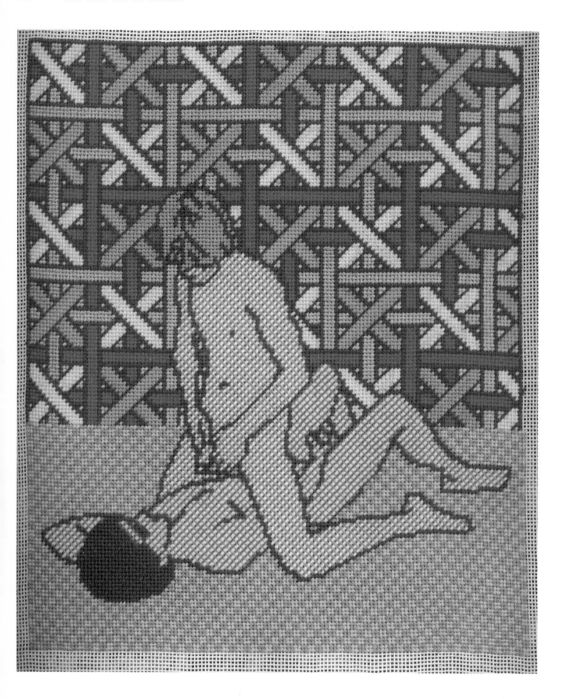

OPPOSITE: Maria E Piñeres, *Pastel Squares*, 2004.
Cotton thread on canvas, 20 x 22.9 cm. Private Collection, Boise, ID. Image courtesy of DCKT Contemporary, NY.

Maria E Piñeres, *Beige Check*, 2004
Cotton thread on canvas, 33 x 27.9 cm. Private collection, San Francisco, CA. Image courtesy of DCKT Contemporary, NY

Maria E Piñeres

Maria E Piñeres has a BFA in illustration from the Parsons School of Design in New York. Her practice is positioned between craft and fine art practices, and evidences the best qualities of both. In the tradition of American Pop Art, Piñeres appropriates images from celebrity portraits and other mass media material, which she juxtaposes against her recreations of familiar craft-based historical iconography. Her work is permeated by an intricate attention to pattern and structure and by the use of fabrics such as plaid, herringbone and houndstooth. "Some of my earliest memories" she explains "are of staring at the floor in my childhood home and being mesmerised by the grids and patterns formed by the coloured tiles. A significant part of my art is about interpreting patterns using the grid of the needlepoint canvas." Most of her background patterns allude to iconic

textile imagery: camouflage, animal skin and flower prints, as well as the 1950s and 60s technicolour designs of Emilio Pucci, Lilly Pulitzer and Vera Neumann.

Piñeres appropriates images of mass appeal—photos of rock idols, film stars and political leaders—in her startlingly faithful representations. Provocative and erotic, her needlework explores the allure of fame and beauty and touches upon themes such as the cult of personality and the myth of the celebrity. *A Rogue's Gallery*, her 2005 exhibition at DCKT Contemporary, features celebrity mug shots portraits. The work alludes to both Kenneth Anger's Hollywood Babylon (a *tour-de-force* into Hollywood's darker side) and *Confidential*, a 1950s LA magazine devoted to scandal, gossip and the misadventures of film stars. "We have been used" Piñeres notes "to seeing celebrities photographed in glamourous

situations, where they have been primped and pampered by crews of professionals. Mug shots however, are candid and extremely real. At first glance, the subject's expressions appear vacant, but on closer inspection, the impression changes. The accused are staring back at authority and their seemingly blank expression are actually full of emotion—sometimes embarrassment, but more often rebelliousness and defiance." In both her working method and her choice of subject, Piñeres evidences an interest in the preconceptions of the popular imagination, electing to explode notions around female identity, sexuality and celebrity with her explicit and expert tapestries.

OPPOSITE: Nava Lubelski, *Spring at the Pole*.
Embroidery, thread on ink-stained canvas, 30.5 x 30.5 cm. Photo: Patrick Lefebvre.

Nava Lubelski, *Clumsy* – detail.
Embroidery, Thread on red wine-stained tablecloth, 79 x 106.7 x 106.7 cm. Photo: Patrick Lefebvre.

Nava Lubelski

Nava Lubelski explores the contradiction between the impulse to destroy and the compulsion to mend. She often hand-stitches over stains, spills and rips in found or ruined linens, or at other times constructs canvases for the purposes of tearing holes through them, marring them with stains or dyes, fashioning injuries to the material which she then 'mends' with her creative method.

~~~~~ *Clumsy*, 2007, is a piece created from a caterer's tablecloth Lubelski salvaged from an art foundation benefit. The tablecloth fell victim to a red wine stain, which the artist 'repaired' aesthetically, elevating mistake to material for artistic consideration. She embroiders the narrative of the random act, and the action that engendered it, by following the extended spread of the stain around its edge, highlighting every splash with hand-stitched red thread. Lubelski contrasts the accidental with the meticulous, using the stain as a 'pattern' from which she creates her abstract forms.

~~~~~ Lubelski considers the social symbolism of the stain, they are the proof or record of a mistake, something shameful or worthy of reproach, that the woman historically cleans up, hides or discards. This traditionally female obligation of order and cleanliness is pitted against another traditionally feminine remit, that of nurturing, mending or caring. Lubelski contrasts these two processes in a creative method that sees the stains nurtured, or fostered, allowed to flourish as intrinsically beautiful forms worthy of artistic attention and exhibition in their own right.

~~~~~ Contrary to this found method is the deliberate act of destroying the fabric or canvas to achieve material injury, purposely creating an outlet for an emotion to

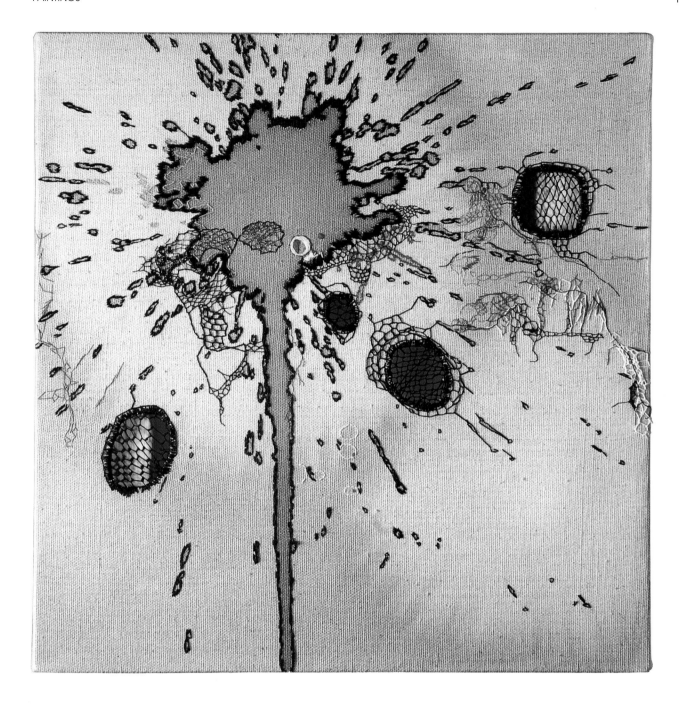

engender. This is itself a mending process by pre-empting a potentially volatile act. This approach is reminiscent of that used by the Abstract Expressionists, a predominantly male movement in painting, which she juxtaposes with masochistic patience and sublimation through considered needlework.

Lubelski continues to visually and emotionally play with creating and mending female sexuality with her canvas pieces. With titles such as *Spring at the North Pole, A Short History, A Lie About Birds* indicating a will to map territory ravaged by conflict, like the aftermath of explosions, containing and connecting areas with boundary lines of coloured thread, attempting to delineate and mend gaps to dam the flow of dried up stains and create a fabric land mass. Lubelski creates a peek-a-boo game with holes and lace latticing a visual landscape that alternately conceals and reveals punctured canvas, fabric or naked frame. War and peace, masculinity and femininity, destruction and construction, exposure and concealment; Lubelski engages these contradictions through celebrating the emotions that engender a variety of human impulses, characteristics and moral challenges.

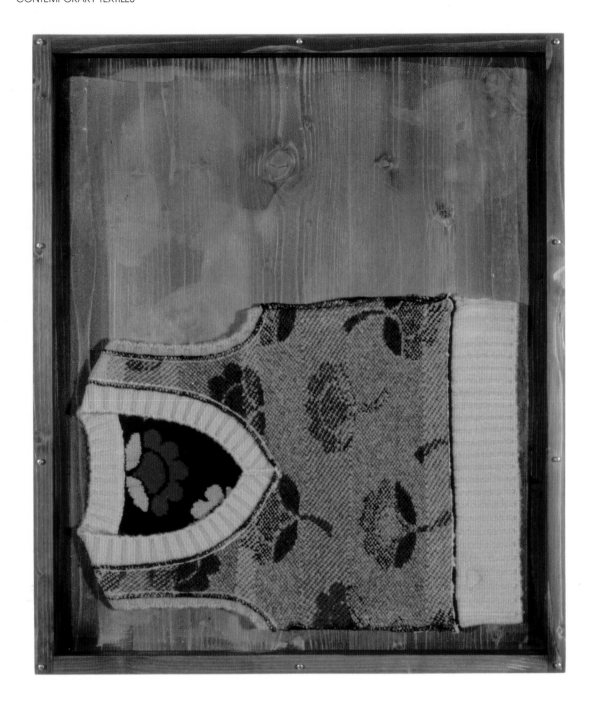

Rosemarie Trockel

German artist Rosemarie Trockel is one of the seminal practitioners to emerge out of Cologne's 1980s art scene and one of the few female artists to gain recognition equivalent to that of canonised German artists such as Gerhard Richter and Sigmar Polke. She has produced an eclectic and challenging body of work over the last two decades, confronting issues such as gender, femininity, desire, popular culture and identity. From her sculptures, to her drawings and oil paintings, Trockel has developed a thoroughly versatile body of work and has often appropriated materials or objects specific to women and the female experience.

~~~~~ In 1985, Trockel started producing her *Strickbilder*, a series of knitted pictures consisting of lengths of machine-knitted woolen material stretched onto frames. Computer-generated logos such as the playboy bunny, the hammer and

sickle and the swastika were endlessly repeated on the surface. A certain chilliness and ironic distance from both conventional notions of femininity and traditionally male artistic pursuits pervade the paintings. Trockel explains: "In the 1970s there were a lot of questionable women's exhibitions, mostly on the theme of house and home. I tried to take wool, which was viewed as a woman's material, out of this context and to rework it in a neutral process of production". The work has since developed into both Trockel's trademark and a landmark in the history of textile art.

~~~~~ Startlingly non-dogmatic, the knitted pictures appeared at a moment when the mechanisms of artistic production and exhibition were dealt with in a sarcastic, ironic or absurd manner. The Mulheimer Freiheit, a group of German artists

influenced by the institutional criticism of Hans Haacke turned the myth of the artistic genius on its head. Trockel shared affinities with the group and treated similar subjects while simultaneously adding an explicitly feminine quality to the work. Her wool pictures lack the dogmatism, force, or monumental energy of Modernist art, unfolding their effect silently and unobtrusively.

Soft and protecting, wool is indeed a material characteristic of her work, with abundant references to weaving and the role of fashion in the construction of identity. *Post-Ménopause*, a 2006 major exhibition at Museum Ludwig in Cologne, opens with a ten metre-wide piece of red woolen threads covering a wall in the museum's foyer; *Yvonne*, 1997, a 12-minute video featuring Trockel's family and friends dressed in afghans, sweaters and knitted pants; *A la Motte*, 1993, a series

of black and white photographs in motion, of a white moth eating a sheet of black knitting. Trockel uses the metaphor of wool to express a variety of themes ranging from the domestic, to the feminine, to the human body, all with her characteristic subtlety and sensitivity.

1. Graw, Isabelle, "Rosemarie Trockel talks to Isabelle Graw—80's Then Interview", *Artforum*, March 2003.

Silja Puranen, *World's strongest man (one hand only)*. Fabric paint, transfer photograph, soft pastel and embroidery on found textile, 198 x 285 cm. Photo: Silja Puranen.

Silja Puranen

Silja Puranen's negotiates the relationship between society and the individual in her work, dealing with the paradigm of social norms and the aesthetic ideal as tools society might use to exercise power or regulate social acceptance. She looks at the specific aesthetics that divide society and rank us as within or outside of the norm.

~~~~~ Puranen digitally manipulates transfer photographs onto found textiles, often deploying autobiographical subject-matter in depicting herself and close relations. She has manipulated images of her own body based on historically changing ideals of beauty to demonstrate the fickle nature of fashion's standards. She has also worked on photographs of herself as a child and places these images in alternative realities, exposing versions of herself with

congenital deficiencies, disabilities or syndromes, which we see in *I could have danced* and *Eats like a bird*, which deal with the conditions of Elephantitus and Anorexia Nervosa in relation to historical and contemporary fashion standards.

~~~~~ Puranen also enjoys referencing illusion and magic, which she uses as metaphors for life, playing with the idea that everything should be glorious and beautiful and that everyone should be young, rich and talented, against the dark side where beautiful things are not always what they seem, often deployed to conceal ugly truths. She chooses her base textiles for the social references they possess and how those latent connotations relate to the subject matter of her work. For example; she uses nightgowns, underwear and bedspreads to play out themes of the feminine.

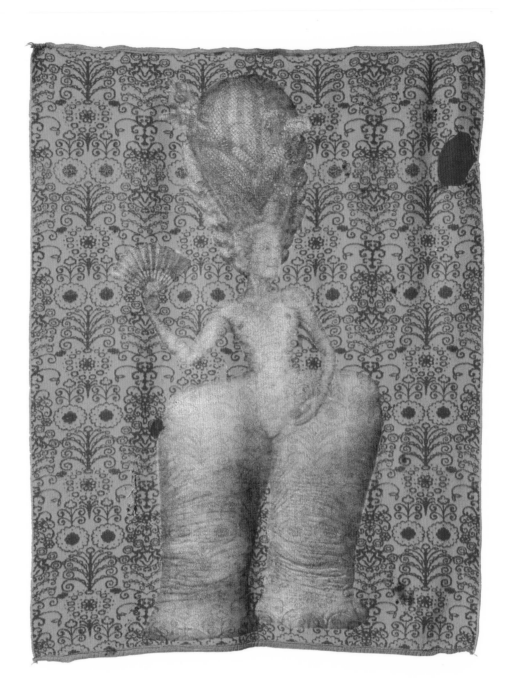

Silja Puranen, *I could have danced all night.*
Fabric paint, transfer photograph and soft pastel on found textile, 180 x 147 cm. Photo: Johnny Korkman.

~~~~~ Puranen's most recent work takes up the imagery of the circus. A place that has a community outside conventional social norms, a place where the people are the objects and the exotic is the everyday, for which she chooses worn out oriental carpets with hand-crafted needlework detail as her base material. She enjoys the kitschy and overwhelmingly romantic character of commercial needlepoint, used metaphorically as much as it is materially.

~~~~~ Puranen is concerned with reversing the norms and the point in popular culture when the relentless pursuit of romantic beauty becomes banal. She uses clothes to reveal what is hidden rather than what is used to cover and protect. Her transfers do not sit on the fabric, but melt into them, exposing the patterns underneath as integral to the applied digital images, encouraging an analogous transparency in the reading of her work. What emerges is an essential dialogue between the subjects Puranen chooses to depict and the material she uses to depict them on, taking up elements of each to build her pictorial narrative.

~~~~~ Puranen's combination of high and low-tech textile techniques expose parallels and divisions between what is considered high and low art. For coloured textiles she has developed a method of painting the fabric, so the image will not totally fade into the background, allowing it to be translucent but distinct, in what can be read as another powerful metaphor, suggestive of relations between the individual and the community, the self and other.

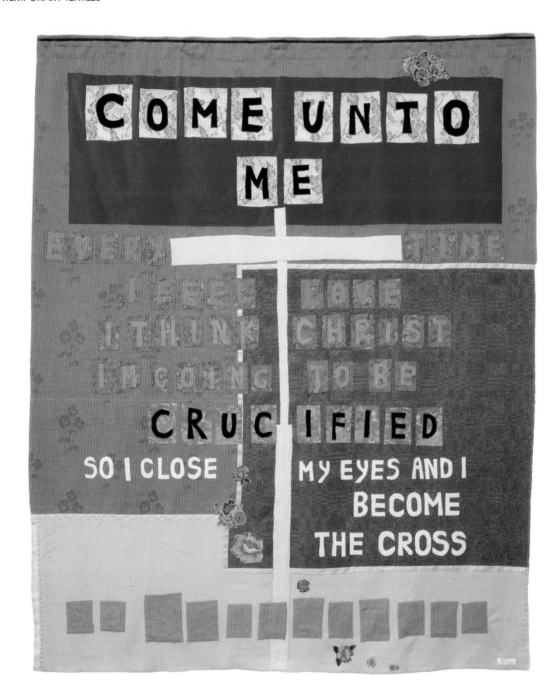

Tracey Emin

Working with an expository autobiographical vocabulary, Tracey Emin has been labelled as everything from a triumph in feminist art and master of turning introspection into spectacle, to a purveyor of vulgarity. One cursory look over the artist's oeuvre, and the viewer is blasted with the striking reality of Emin's disturbingly entertaining biography. Emin completely eradicates the divide between reality and art; the viewer is forced to see each work as a material representation of Emin and her life. As one of the most poignant examples of an artist of the 'personal as the political', Emin includes anything and everything about herself in her artwork; exploring sex, anger, love, drunkenness, rape, abortion, and family, nothing is too intimate. Often heralded as an icon of post-feminism through her blunt appropriations of vulgarity, Emin subsequently allies the unspeakable with a notably feminine manifestation of sexuality. Appropriating quilting and craft, and by marrying the explicitly sexual and the feminine ornamental aesthetic, Emin attempts to turn conventional notions of femininity upside down. Although the bright colours and adolescent handwriting often give her work an air of puerility, the overtly direct sexual subject matter forces the viewer to reconsider her work within a new vocabulary. Using tapestries as the metaphorical pages of her autobiography, Emin stitches together felt letters into words (often misspelled and even more frequently expletives), and brightly coloured patches of cloth or stereotypically feminine floral swatches of fabric. She divulges her deepest and darkest secrets through paintings, sculptures, books, poetry, drawings, photography and video installations, as she constantly

Tracey Emin, *Helter Fucking Skelter*, 2001. Applique blanket, 253 x 220 cm. © The artist. Image courtesy of Jay Jopling/ White Cube (London). Photo: Stephen White.

explores new ways to exorcise her emotions and express them through her creative practice.

~~~~~ As a member of the ever contentious Young British Artists, Emin's work for the Royal Academy's *Sensation* exhibition, *Everyone I Ever Slept With*, brought her to the forefront as a major contender in the world of contemporary art. On the interior fabric of a blue igloo-shaped tent, Emin appliquéd patches of felt letters, spelling out the names of everyone she had ever shared a bed with. Emin included not only the names of her past lovers, but also the names of family members, friends, and her aborted foetus. Because the embroidery was attached to the interior of the tent, the viewer was required to crawl into the tent and lie down, almost mimicking a child at play.

~~~~~ Emin's keenly adept (whether intentional or not) ability to promote herself has not only caught the eye of famed collector Charles Saatchi, but also saw her shortlisted for the Turner Prize. Emin's work undeniably shook convention from the very beginning, yet the artist quickly became a celebrity in the art world when she appeared drunk on a 1997 BBC Channel 4 Turner Prize debate. Although the incident could have changed the course of her career for the worse, Emin's knack for exposing her self-destruction soon proved positive. 'Tracey Emin' has fast become a household name.

OPPOSITE: Wendy Huhn, *Conversation.*
Canvas, paint couching, paint, heat transfers, 46 x 55 cm. Photo: David Loveall Photography Inc.

Wendy Huhn, *Thantaphobia*
Hand-embroidery with cotton, beads, silk flowers, 19 x 19 cm. Photo: David Loveall Photogtaphty Inc.

Wendy Huhn

Wendy Huhn works in textiles, collage and mixed media. She superimposes imagery on painted and sanded canvases or small hand-embroidered collages, using everything from vintage fabrics, beads, horsehair nets and images cut-out from magazines. Huhn finds inspiration in the everyday, the banal, unpicking the extraordinary from the objects that often blend into the background of modern experience. "Inspiration comes to me from everyday situations I find people engaged in…. I borrow imagery from eighteenth and nineteenth century women's magazines and books. While culling, cutting, and combining from my sources, I attempt to play the historical images against modern day culture".[1]

~~~~~ One of the most appealing and engaging aspects of Huhn's art is her expert feel for colour and composition. She creates intricate, exquisitely balanced relationships that draw a variety of seemingly disparate visual signifiers into a riotous harmony with one another. The entire picture plane somehow functions as a coherent assemblage, though it is comprised of a language of countless unrelated symbols and structures.

~~~~~ "The stories I tell through my work reflect the way I view the world— often a brash voice in a room of hushed tones" Huhn explains.[2] She does not shy away from the decorative in her creative approach, rather she chooses to work within its constraints to upset its connotations; that is, her ornamental style coupled with her unusual choice of subject matter, forces an uneasy reading of her work as somehow simultaneously within and outside of craft or fine art, taking up a hotly debated argument recurrent in art textile.

~~~~~ Huhn's work recalls children's drawings, the art of Henry Darger and other folk or non-institutionalised art, reminiscent of a tradition of resistance in the history of fine art practice, a refusal to be contained by the conventions of high art. Precision and amplitude of detail, use of bright hues and filled contours and references to primitivism and children's books are common aspects of her creative approach throughout her oeuvre.

1. Taken from the artist's statement, submitted to the author in October 2007.
2. Taken from the artist's statement, submitted to the author in October 2007.

SCUL

TURES

Annet Couwenberg, *Ruffled Collar*, 2004. Nomex crepe paper, millinery wire, hoop-steel, 30 x 792.5 x 671 cm.

Annet Couwenberg

Annet Couwenberg, has spent her life straddled between America and The Netherlands. This has meant that her life and work has been spread across two continents and influenced by two different social reforms. She says her traditions are in the Dutch civic responsibility and a work ethic tempered by socialism and the constraints of Calvinism. This contrasts with her experience of America, where individuality is often celebrated over community.

~~~~~ Couwenberg looks at the fine line between restrictive social norms and private desires in her work, for which she uses clothes as a metaphor. Her quest for self-determination and dependency is a personal one and the driving force behind her work. She uses clothing details such as ruffles and bows as social references to beauty ideals, oversizing, stacking and placing them on the floor, she abstracts the forms so they appear as self-contained organic structures. Reminiscent of obsolete Elizabethan masculine and feminine ideals, from a distance, the structures also appear as hollow female forms. The word "enough" embroidered onto a skin-coloured centre initiates an open-ended dialogue about value, identity and social norms.

~~~~~ *Discarded Ruffled Collar*, is a shedding and abstracting of both ruffs, bows, collars and ties in a white and red palette. The ruffs are the precarious edges of starched conformity, weighed down by their oversized re-creation and hung by white ties, suggesting individuality residing over social dependency.

~~~~~ She believes that, through the analogy of clothing as our shelter, fabric is a material can allow us to address our understanding of self and culture: becoming a place of introspection, a place to explore what we are, what we

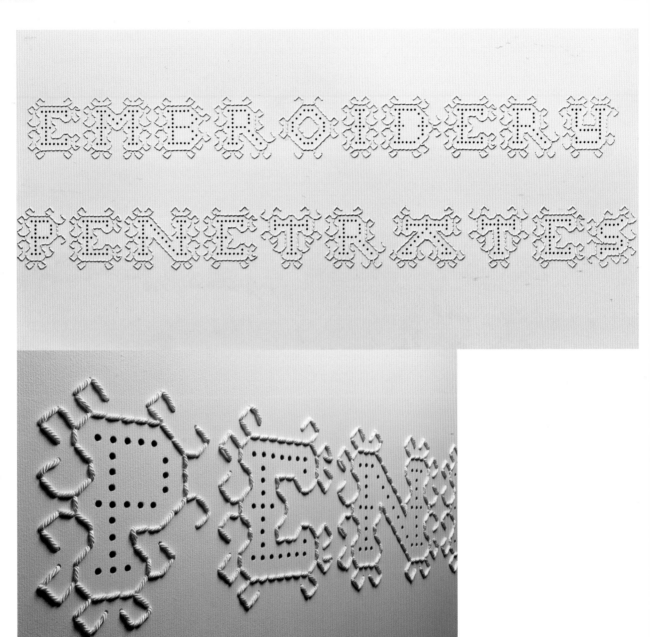

Annet Couwenberg, *Embroidery Penetrates*, 2007.
Embroidered through wall, twisted cord, MDF panel, drilled holes.

Annet Couwenberg, *Embroidery Penetrates*, 2007.
Embroidered through wall, twisted cord, MDF panel, drilled holes.

Annet Couwenberg, *Embroidery Penetrates*, detail, 2007.
Embroidered through wall, twisted cord, MDF panel, drilled holes.

have learnt to be and what we desire. Like many artists working with textiles, Couwenberg's work revolves around gender issues, the value of tradition and the compulsion to conform. Her choice is mostly undergarments indicative of private desires but shown as restrictive corsets and bustles that dictate the shape of women's bodies, literally forcing organic forms into social criteria of beauty and sexual value.

~~~~~ More recently, Couwenberg discovered the potential of computerised embroidery machines in her work, which she programs to stitch her own digitally forged designs. She is so convinced by its promise that she has urged the Maryland Institute's College of Art, where she chairs the Textile Department, to buy three more such machines for the use of the students.

~~~~~ As in her previous practice, Couwenberg's developing digital work deals with repetition of the symbolic image; the corset in different colours, sizes, stitch patterns, orientations. Once again, the themes of conformity, identity and the feminine play out in a grand theatre of multiple social signifiers.

Annette Messager, *articulés-désarticulés*, 2002.
Fabric puppets, automatic engines, cables, wooden sticks, fabric columns, projectors, 5,600 cm x 1,500 x 1,400 cm. Collection of the Musée National d'Art Moderne, Centre Pompidou.

Annette Messager, *Doomestic*, 2000
Fabrics, thread, 300 x 335 x 30 cm. Collection of the Musée d'Art moderne de la Ville de Paris.

Annette Messager

Annette Messager in one of the most prolific and influential artists of her generation. She was born in Berck, France, during 1943 and lives and works in Malakoff, a suburb of Paris. Messager trained as an artist at the Ecole Nationale Supérieure des Arts Décoratifs in Paris, but she abandoned her studies, and with a group of like minded artists—Christian Boltanski, Gina Pane and Jean Le Gac—engaged in a practice that was in tune with the socio-political upheavals of late 1960s France. Since then she has been creating work that deals with themes of power, the body, sexuality, gender and the grotesque. Her practice has encompassed drawing, painting, embroidery, collage, sculpture and even writing.

~~~~ Messager's approach to art-making has favoured the everyday, the domestic and the quotidian: she has used a wide range of materials to fashion her works, from nets, found objects, toys and coloured pencils to crayons, stockings, newspaper clippings and cloth. Her sources have been equally diverse: Man Ray, the surrealist Claude Cahun, Jean Genet, outsider art, Sol LeWitt, alchemy, witchcraft and astrology. Messager deliberately blurs boundaries between the high and low, realism and the fantastic and the private and the public. Mixing influences and forms, her work emerges as a carnival of imagery that rejects all established hierarchies and structures. "Conceptual art interests me" she claims "in the same way as the art of the insane, astrology and religious art. It's not the ideologies which these areas perpetuate that interest me: they are for me, above all else, repertories of forms. I make fun of sorcery and alchemy even if I make full use of their signs."[1]

Annette Messager, *Rumeur,* 2000–2004, fabrics, plush pieces, threads, 100 x 235 x 43 cm. Collection of Marin Karmitz, Paris.

Annette Messager

~~~~~~ The theme of duality has underpinned Messager's practice from the outset. When asked to participate in a wool-themed exhibition in 1971 at the Galerie Germain, she decided to submit a taxidermied sparrow wrapped in a knitted covering. This marked the beginning of a series of works that juxtapose soft, concealing and non-threatening materials with a rather disquieting subject matter. *Victim of Torture,* features a teddy bear bound with black netting and hanged upside down; *Doomestic* is a mountain of stuffed puppets that are bound, mutated and altered beyond recognition. In Messager's work, objects are continually altered to change their essential nature, pencils become weapons, dolls become monsters and the home a stage of cruelty, culminating in a fascinating study of the unconscious anxieties lurking in the popular imaginary.

1. Messager quoted in Bernard Marcade's "Annette Messager" *Bomb 26,* Winter 1988/1989.

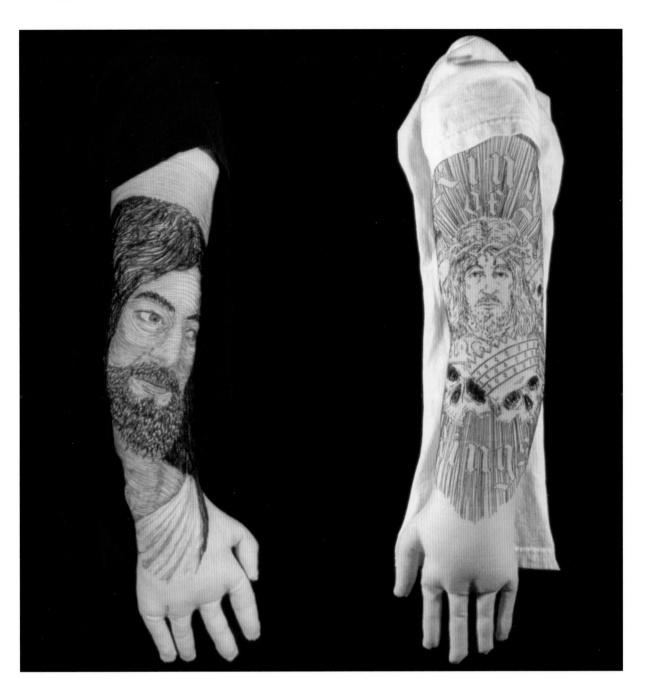

LEFT: Benji Whalen, *Jesus Christ*, 2007.
Embroidery floss on stuffed cotton, cotton sleeve, 54 cm long.
RIGHT: Benji Whalen, *King of Kings*, 2006.
Embroidery floss on stuffed cotton, cotton sleeve, 53 cm long.

Benji Whalen

San Francisco-based artist Benji Whalen works in painting, sculpture and embroidery. A visit to his grandmother's house triggered his interest in needlework and he soon began creating his alphabet quilts; a series of embroidered images stitched onto unassembled patchworks of fabric, with each image illustrating a letter of the alphabet. Often humourous or ironic, these embroideries introduce a sinister subject-matter to an otherwise innocent medium paving the way for Whalen's recent work, a series of stuffed fabric arms embellished with tattoo embroideries, rich with allusions to counter-cultural, transgressive lifestyles.

~~~~~ Whalen grew up among a community of artists—the Bread and Puppet Theatre in Vermont—and this background informs the ethos behind, and the character of, his recent fabric sculptures. Whalen's tattoo embroideries have an arresting simplicity that is at odds with the over-conceptualised, self-referential work typical of contemporary artistic practice. He alludes to and appropriates techniques ostracised from the traditional art canon—tattooing, puppetry, embroidery, all activities with a subversive potential. Puppetry was considered a remnant from pagan societies and was once banished by the Church; tattoos have served as marks of outcasts, slaves and convicts; embroidery became, in the hands of artists such as Rosemarie Trockel, Elaine Reichek and Ghada Amer, an instrument of resistance and subversion. Whalen draws parallels between all three elements, fusing the masculine with the feminine, the soft with the hard, the decorative with the conceptual.

OPPOSITE: Guerra de la Paz, *Ring Around the Rosy*, 2006.
Mixed media sculptural installation with children's camouflage garments, shoes, bowling ball, rope, wood, Irregular, approximately 152 x 152 x 122 cm. Private Collection.

Guerra de la Paz, *Snake Charmer*, 2007.
Mixed media sculpture with garments, shoes, form, wood, approximately 182.9 x 61 x 48 cm.

Guerra de la Paz

Guerra de la Paz represents the collaborative efforts of Cuban-born artists Alain Guerra and Neraldo de la Paz. They have been working together for more than 11 years, experimenting with a variety of formats and creating provocative large-scale installations. In *Ring Around the Rosy*, a group of children perform a disturbing ritual, circled in dance around a bomb; elsewhere references to Michelangelo's *Pieta* enter into a dialogue with themes of struggle, victory and death. Their work references and reinterprets—classic symbolism while pricking at present conflicts and events.

~~~~~ The duo's primary material is the discarded object. Consistent throughout their practice is the use of found fabrics collected from piles of unwanted clothing. "We are fascinated by the ability to refashion someone's junk into a piece of fine art and how refuse as a material can add spiritual energy and historic reference."[1] These very personal materials, the left over and the discarded, evidence a culture of mass consumption, where people and things can be cast aside in favour of some fleeting desire or ambition.

~~~~~ "Our future goals remain consistent in that we wish to continue our focus on experimentation and the visual language we have established. Consciously reinventing ourselves while expanding our exploration of the human condition and merging materials both traditional and non-traditional."[2]

1. Taken from the artist's statement, submitted to the author in November 2007.
2. Taken from the artist's statement, submitted to the author in November 2007.

OPPOSITE: Gyöngy Laky, *Globalisation II: Homogenization*, 2004.
Apple, commercial wood, plastic soldiers, sheet rock screws and bullets for building, 81 × 246 × 122 cm.

Gyöngy Laky, *Bottom Line*, 2005.
Charcoal, bullets for building, black caulking, plastic soldiers, 84 × 56 × 122. Photo: Ben Blackwell.

Gyöngy Laky

Gyöngy Laky is widely known for her sculptural constructions, referred to as textile architecture. She has built an international reputation exhibiting cross-culturally from France, Spain and Lithuania to Columbia, China and the Philippines. In America, where Laky immigrated to as a child, she has cemented a position as a key textile artist. Characterised by her poetic sculptures that voice discontent with society's careless attitude to the environment, her work is currently represented in number of permanent collections across America.

~~~~~ Working with ostensibly waste materials, discarded by society, she builds sculptural forms using simple, direct methods of construction that question the notion of waste in today's throw-away culture. Either using humble, organic materials such as tree debris to reference the versatility of nature, or in taking man-made items such as nails, food skewers, toothpicks and golf tees to elevate the human values of ingenuity, flexibility and imagination she endeavours to use the inherent optimism in making things to promote the possibility of harmony between nature and humanity.

~~~~~ Her interest in the universality of symbols runs through her work, stemming from a mixed background, which brought her into contact with many languages and cultures. In using words, symbols and icons as sculptures she draws on their efficacy to comment effectively on universal issues beyond her immediate concerns. In recent years her work has taken up a polemical stance as she incorporates plastic babies and soldiers to voice opposition to continued gender inequality and the wasteful strategies of war used by the American government.

Janet Cooper, Assemblage Party Dress from my travels to Rome, France and Japan, 2007.
83.8 x 81.3 x 5.1 cm.

Janet Cooper

Janet Cooper's work is a visual riot of feminine signifiers. Taking up the narrative of the domestic, Cooper creates careful studies of women's work and culture using traditional methods of production.

~~~~~ "I am in love with the patinas of the used and the mysteries of the discarded. I am intrigued by the mechanics and precision of women's work: sewing, crocheting, knitting and quilting. I treasure the themes of memory and the common place."[1]

~~~~~ Cooper's work reads like an encyclopaedia elaborating the characteristics of female life, including everything from discarded dolls, to sewing implements and scraps of disused clothing and paper culled from flea markets and rubbish bins. Cooper's fascination with a shared female history runs a consistent theme through her varied bricolage works, often choosing to stich, quilt, knit or crochet

the ephemera she finds into something like a story of what it means to be a girl. Her work underlines the sentiment that women share something by virtue of being taught these particularly female skills, and by being exposed to these specifically female toys, accessories and adornments. These objects in some sense represent the history of the female, and Cooper's works hang together in what feels like an open-ended, unfinished account of that shared experience.

~~~~ In her *Party Dresses* series, Cooper fashions mock garments out of a collection of cross-cultural objects ranging from Indian fabrics, old sewing patters, buttons, straight pins, coins, reels of thread and photographs. She uses all of the raw material of the seamstress, but employs them in surprising ways, making the viewer highly aware of their materiality, their symbolism and their

Janet Cooper, *A Dress Honoring Darkness and Anxiety*, 2007.
106 x 91 x 50 cm.

cultural significance. For example, Cooper rouches old sewing patterns and uses them as petticoats, she applies bobbins, reels and pins as haberdashery adorning her garments, rather as the material that invisibly binds them together. These tools that are traditionally silent in a finished piece of sewing or quilting are expressed as important in their own right, interesting for their form and meaning and worthy of exhibition.

~~~~ It is this sentiment that underlines Cooper's fascination with a cultural past common to the female realm. In bringing the accoutrements of women's work out of the seams and into view, positioning them as intrinsically valuable and beautiful, Cooper elaborates on the value and beauty of what is often thought of as mundane domestic labour.

1. From the artist's statement, http://www.art-e-zine.co.uk/janet.html, retrieved 2 February 2008.

Janet Echelman, *She Changes*, 2005. Waterfront plaza, Porto and Matosinhos, Portugal. Tenara® PTFE architectural fiber, 50 X 150 X 150 m. Image courtesy Joao Ferrand, www.echelman.com.

Janet Echelman

Janet Echelman is a transformer of urban airspace. Fashioning larger-than-life wind sculptures, Echelman solicits the help of a whole host of architects, engineers, consultants and planners to install massive structures of rope and steel in, often unlikely, urban settings These sculptures are designed to respond to their environments, to change with the wind and rain, to move and be moved in a fundamental sitedness that forever marries Echelman's work with the landscape in which it exists.

~~~~~ Echelman began her practice as a painter, and it wasn't until she caught sight of a volume of fishing nets on the beach during a trip to India that she began to consider a change in creative approach. "It was during a trip to India in 1997 as a Fulbright Senior Lecturer in Painting. I had shipped paints, but as the deadline for my show approached and my paints didn't, I realised I had a problem. In the meantime, every afternoon I would walk to the beach for a swim and watch the fishermen, fascinated by the way they folded their lengths of net into large volumes. It suddenly dawned on me that this was a different way to approach volume, and I was re-born as a sculptor."[1]

~~~~~ It was this shift that prompted Echelman to work in textile, taking up the language of the vernacular in her site-specific work. In devising a piece for a particular site, she considers the visual language of the surrounding region, the methods of making common to its inhabitants and the use the community makes of the site itself, taking these principles as the starting point for her creative method.

Janet Echelman, *She Changes*, 2005. Waterfront plaza, Porto and Matosinhos, Portugal, Tenara® PTFE architectural fiber, 50 X 150 X 150 m. Image Courtesy Joao Ferrand, www.echelman.com.

~~~~~~ *She Changes* is a monumental red and white netted structure sited along the shorelines in the town of Matosinhos, just outside of Porto. The structure itself is massive, 20 tons of rope and cable, suspended by a steel rim connected to three diagonally-placed poles, each measuring anywhere from 25 to 50 metres in height. The construction of the piece enlisted the help of a dedicated team of architects, planners, fabricators, landscape designers, IT specialists and, of course, the careful planning and management of the artist herself. Made from an architectural fibre called Tenara®, the material was chosen to withstand exposure to sun, wind and sea salty air. The design was devised in Paris using a specialised software, and was sent to Washington for fabrication, the resulting materials thereafter shipped to the site in large parcels.

~~~~~ The effect is monumental. A mass of vibrant, billowing netting that ebbs and flows with the force of the wind, changing colour and character with the cycles of day and night. The material itself is suggestive of the fishing nets that have played a historically important role in the community of Porto and its surrounding regions. The piece articulates a conversation with the physical and social landscape of its site, forever changing in response to its environment.

1. The artist discussing *She Changes* in conversation with Lilly Wei, http://www.sculpture.org/documents/scmag05/julaug_05/echelman.shtml, retrieved 1 February 2008.

Jann Haworth

Female artists are barely given fair representation in the exhibition space in the twenty-first century, but when Jann Haworth was working as a fine artist nearly 50 years ago, it was close to impossible to be taken seriously as an artist in Britain's male-dominated art scene. It is therefore curious, and commendable, that she chose to work with fabric, a traditionally female medium that would have reminded her peers of the domestic work so associated with the female mind at the time.

~~~~~ This choice was not made without contention and critique from her fellows, indeed when Eduardo Paolozzi saw Haworth's *Cowboy* he famously said "cast it in bronze" to which Haworth replied "I had cast it in cloth and that was the point".[1] Faced with the sexism rampant in post-war Britain's art scene,

Haworth use of fabric was ironic, employing a language and a medium that was opaque to her male peers, but ideal for expressing the malleability of the female creative mind, and the surprisingly serious objects it could produce.

~~~~~ Jann Haworth was born in Los Angeles in 1942, her mother was part of a Californian group of silk-screen artists and her father was a production designer in Hollywood. In 1961, she moved to London to attend a fine art course at The Slade, marrying fellow artist Peter Blake in 1963. As many female artists of this time or that, Haworth became associated with Blake's life and work rather than acknowledged for her own. However, she remained undeterred, and the flippancy with which her potential was viewed only served to deepen her resolve to employ fabric as medium. "I was annoyed enough, and American enough, to

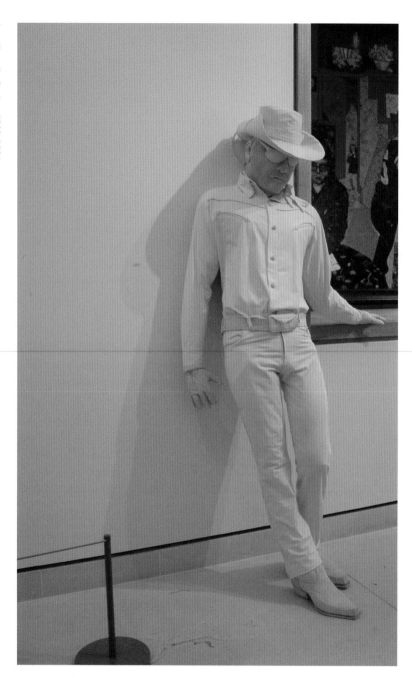

Jann Haworth, *Cowboy*, 1963–1964.
180 cm high, kapok and unbleached calico. Pallant House Gallery, Wilson Gift through the Art Fund. © The artist.

Jann Haworth

take that on. I was determined to better them, and that's one of the reasons for the partly sarcastic choice of cloth, latex and sequins as media. It was a female language to which the male students didn't have access."

~~~~~ *Cowboy* is a life-sized sculpture elaborating Haworth's impressions of life in the southern states of America during the 1950s and 60s. She was struck by the racial segregation and sexism coursing through the culture at the time, taking up the image of the cowboy as a metaphor for the conflict she felt whilst visiting that part of the world. The image of the cowboy was simultaneously an attractive and seductive figure and an uneducated, prejudiced villain, which may have prompted Haworth to use the unlikely medium of fabric to highlight the absurdity of the heroically tough cowboy persona.

~~~~~ As in her life and work, Haworth's daring use of textiles in a fine art context flew in the face of all expectation, choosing to ignore the ambivalence to her capacity and instead practicing fine art in a specifically female way. She continues to push the boundaries of critical categories of artistic practice, and is due credit for being one of the first fine artists to engage with textile as a material worthy of conceptual attention.

1. Stevens, Chris. "Still Swinging after all these Years? Art and the 60s: This Was Tomorrow" *Tate Etc.* Issue 1, Summer 2004, Tate Publishing: London, 2004.

Dave Cole, *The Knitting Machine*, 2005.
Installation, knitting large flag. Massachusetts Museum of Contemporary Art.

Dave Cole

Dave Cole takes the use of textiles to monumental proportions in his installation work. Using industrial materials and machinery, Cole knits incredibly large installation pieces that hyperbolise the act to such an extent that it becomes something different altogether, something strange and nearly magical.

~~~~~ Knitting is generally associated with the domestic; quiet, mundane work to be done in the home, but through a drastic increase in scale, Cole manages to make knitting a spectacle, and an exciting one at that. In an installation at the Massssachusetts Museum of Contemporary Art that verged on performance art, Cole enlisted the help of two yellow John Deere excavators each fitted with seven and a half meter aluminium light poles that served as oversized knitting needles. Cole, and his assistant Joel Taplin, stood on a boom over nine metres

off of the ground and used a long fishing gaff to cast a considerable length of red, white and blue felt over the 'needles'. in a transfixing demonstration of careful planning, the artist managed to knit a seven meter-wide American flag in less than 24 hours, attracting the curiosity of a small group of people who had gathered to watch this extraordinary piece unfold.

~~~~~ It is this grand scale that Cole has become most associated with, taking the principles of a domestic craft and bringing them very much into the public sphere, radicalising his method through sheer size and mechanisation, and thereby completely changing the nature of knitting and its known associations.

OPPOSITE: Laura Ford, *Headthinker IV*, 2003. Steel, plaster, ceramic, fabric, shelves, 145 x 330 x 45 cm. Image courtesy of the artist and Houldsworth Gallery, London.

Laura Ford, *Elephant Boy 2*, 1999. Steel, wool, plaster, 106 cm (high). Image courtesy of the artist and Houldsworth, London.

Laura Ford

Laura Ford has developed an idiosyncratic yet coherent body of work, characterised by the negotiation of potent and vital socio-political themes through the discomforting combination of figurative sculpture, an acerbic humour, and melancholic, often sinister, associations. The protagonists of her sculptural installations are bizarre cross-breeds or hybrid creatures: potentially anthropomorphic beasts, they tread ambiguously the line between the real and the fictitious, inertness and active power, innocence and corruption.

~~~~~ It is this deployment of an equivocal and pluralistic strategy that, perhaps paradoxically, defines the particular cogency of the creatures that inhabit Ford's uncanny world. Her 2004 exhibition, *Wreckers,* consisted of a group of small figures, ostensibly children, 'dressed' head-to-toe in plain fabric and who seemed to be making their way through the gallery space. But there is something unsettling about these figures—they all have cloth packs of dynamite strapped to them. Among them stands a colossal and dominating female figure—a bearded lady with 'home-made' medals pinned to her all-black clothes—an at once protective and terrifying, maternal and authoritarian force. Here, children no longer simply play at war, dancers' bells instead signal an oncoming 'suicide' bomb: they are at once heroes and freedom fighters. Ford deftly manipulates commonplace fabrics to complicate the viewer's instincts towards these characters: khaki cloth denotes no party with which to align oneself, and black twill carries suggestions not only of blankness and neutrality but of religious dress, the uniform of terrorist or paramilitary groups.

~~~~~ Ford's *Chintz Girls,* made originally in 1998, a group of petticoated girls with plaited hair covered entirely in floral printed cotton, stand animatedly on circular rugs. However, these apparently innocuous figures are strangely contorted, arms bent back, to become part dancing-child, part deformed jewellery-box ballerina, awkwardly—and perhaps distressingly—fixed to the floor. Sickly-sweet, the cheerfulness of these girls in their chintz is suddenly and drastically undermined by the violence of their positioning; in this work as in others, Ford probes the boundaries of societal control and human power, and the notions of innocence in childhood and rationalism in adulthood.

~~~~~ Another series, *Headthinker,* 2003, consists of several small boys who carry a cumbersome and exhausting weight upon their shoulders, in the form of oversized ceramic donkey's heads, a burden too great to carry for any length of time. Weary and prostrate, these boys in men's clothes enact a half-hearted exhibitionism in which they rest against or prop up the slick shelves and plinths of a white-cube gallery space. Contiguously melancholy Eeyores or miniature visions of the absurd Bottom character from Shakespeare, they have found a place to sleep, or an object to bang their heads against, in the confines and specificities of the gallery structure. It is Ford's sardonically humourous undertones that ensure that the plurality of her works is motivated along an always circular path: turning every reference or interpretation back on itself, she reveals the paradoxes, transgressions and myths that define, and indeed justify, the social and political histories of our world.

OPPOSITE: Lucy + Jorge Orta, *Connector-Mobile Village I*, 2001.
Aluminium-coated polyester, reversible Soklen Lycra, open-cell polyurethane, Silkscreen print, zips, 570x700 cm. Image courtesy of the artists.
Lucy + Jorge Orta, *Nexus Architecture x 50-Nexus Type Opera tion VII*, 2001.
Performance for 50 dancers. Collaboration with Markus & Simon Stockhausen, Annamirl van der Pluij, Köln, Germany. Image courtesy of the artists.

Lucy + Jorge Orta

Lucy + Jorge Orta use textiles to employ a totally unique method of art-making, framing their work as a radical description of the role of art in the machinery of social policy.

~~~~~ The Ortas' work is based on collaboration, not just in the making, but also in the exhibition and explanation of what is ultimately a process-based creative approach. Founding Studio Orta in 1991, the two artists have focused on the potential of the artistic method to underline serious social and political issues alive in international community. Through their collaboration with curators, designers, architects, engineers, musicians, artisans, fabricators, production assistants and technicians, the Ortas have facilitated the production of large-scale interactions between numerous individuals,

producing fascinating textiles-based constructions in an irreversible fusing of process and outcome.

~~~~~ Trained in fashion and textiles in Nottingham, the beginning of Lucy's artistic practice coincided with her awareness of a particularly complicated time in international politics. With the fall of the Berlin Wall, the remapping of eastern Europe, the end of the Cold War and the beginning of the Gulf War, Lucy Orta's artistic outlook was inextricably linked to a period of political uncertainty and cultural unrest. Her burgeoning fashion career brought her to Paris, where she met artist and architect Jorge Orta at an opening of one of his gallery shows in 1991. Frustrated by the fashion scene's lack of political discourse, Lucy soon joined Jorge's collective at the Bastille studios, sparking a greater awareness of

the potential for the creative process to impact upon social issues and marking the beginning of her migration from fashion to the world of contemporary art. Lucy + Jorge Orta have been working together as collaborators ever since, but as they describe, their artistic method differs greatly from the conventional, notion of the solitary creative mind. Rather, the Ortas behave more like facilitators, conductors of a grand orchestra where the aims and talents of countless contributors are steadily refined through constant collaboration, eventually expressed through one action, event or object.

~~~~~ *Nexus Architecture* investigates the possibility of a renewed potential for artistic social action through precisely these methods. The Ortas have facilitated the creation of a network of body sculptures that function both as individual forms

Lucy + Jorge Orta, *Connector Mobile Village and Body Architecture – Foyer D.* 2001–2002. Installation at The Fabric Workshop, Philadelphia, 900 x 200 x 260 cm. Private collection, Brussels.

Lucy + Jorge Orta

and as a community of structures, suggestive of the solidarity of protest. The silver jumpsuits worn by the participants in Köln, stencilled with words such as "heart", "nexus" and "fraternité", are linked by fabric filaments, fastening the interventionists together in a spectacle of collaboration and community. Lucy's background in fashion and textiles and Jorge's beginnings as a social activist in South America, are woven together in a fascinating dialogue expressed through the mass action of no less than 50 multicultural, multi-lingual and multi-limbed participants standing in a grid, forming an imposing metaphor for the possibility of unity and community in uncertain political times.

~~~~ The *Connector* project evidences a similar set of ambitions, where the Ortas have travelled to several different locations and situations around the world to perform extended actions or interventions with a group of individuals. One such group was found at the Robert Gifford Psychiatric Hospital in Québec City, where the Ortas collaborated with patients and faculty to produce an interconnected body sculpture, linking six or more people into a sleeping-bag survival structure, suggestive of mutual reliance and the necessity of community.

~~~~ The use of textiles is at the heart of the Ortas' practice, its malleability and flexibility are absolutely essential to the kind of interconnected fluidity that typifies the artists' work. Using these structures and situations, the Ortas' understand collaborative artistic practice as a tool to bring serious humanitarian issues to the forefront of the creative method.

Lucy + Jorge Orta, *Siamese Armour*, 2003–2004.
Army campbed linen, rope, eyelets, variable dimensions.

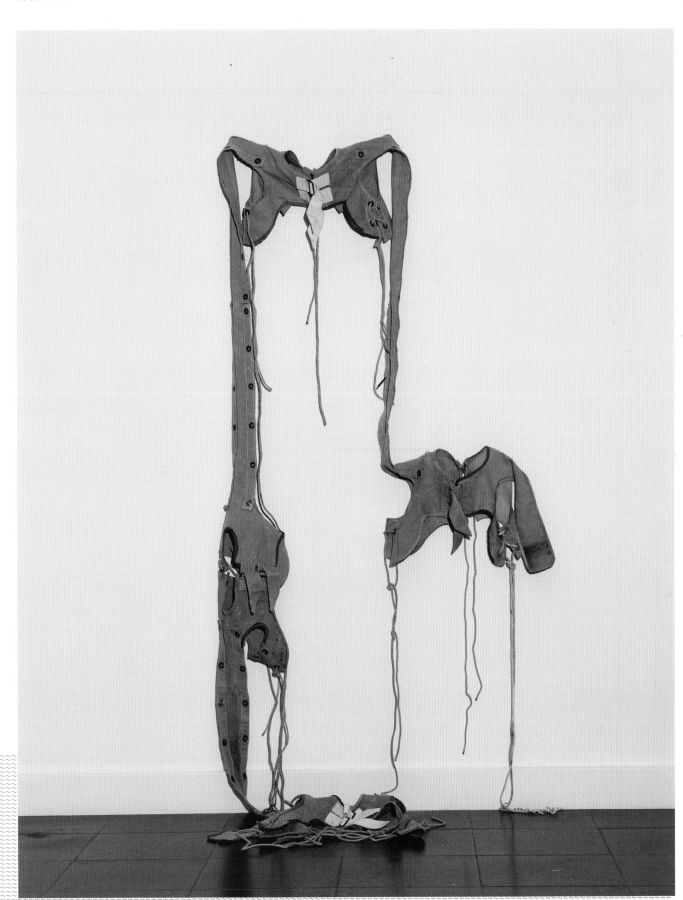

Susan Taber Avila, *Garden (detail)*, 2006. Thread, digitally printed silk on industrial felt, machine stitching, 229 x38 x 11.4 cm. Photo: Lee Fatherree.

Susan Taber Avila

Susan Taber Avila's work plays with notions of identity and containment. She uses the medium of textiles as an allegory for language, for the pure potential expressed in the identities we articulate through adornment. In choosing a particular manner of dress or costume, we choose to present ourselves to the world in a particular way. Avila's work therefore underlines how our personalities or ambitions are communicated through the vessel of textiles, how the way we frame ourselves physically betrays something of how we frame our identities in a larger sense: "The textile medium replaces language for describing an event, a place, or a memory."[1] In her *Shoe Stories*, Avila explores the nature of footwear as a container for identity, taking up stereotypes and associations with particular modes of dress, and critically repositioning them to create a dialogue with the concepts

these personal objects have been historically used to describe. Not only does Avila often choose subjects traditionally made from fabric or other pliable materials, but she represents them using that same class of medium, fashioning a running shoe from quilted fabric, or using an industrial felt and sewing machine to build a French courtier's high heel. The resulting objects are simultaneously immediately available to the viewer because of their form and placed at a distance by virtue of their construction, opening up the space for the critical view Avila seeks to encourage.

1. Susan Taber Avila, "*Shoe Stories* Artist Statement" www.suta.com, retrieved 2 February 2008.

What's the password?

Mark Newport, *Password*.
Archival ink jet print, 48 x 33 cm. Image courtesy of the artist.

Mark Newport

"I work to forge the link between childhood experience and adult understanding of protection, masculinity, and heroism."[1]

~~~~~ Mark Newport's knitted superhero costumes question masculinity. These characters represent idealised maleness to children—as father figures and aspirational adulthood incarnations—through their fictionalised personas. The connotations of the heroic, protective, ultra-male forms are subverted when they are rendered in the traditionally female medium of knitted structures. These icons of macho, invincible strength—Batman, Spiderman, even Captain America—become vulnerable, lifeless forms as the rippling muscles of the hero beneath are removed. Through the soft, visually pleasing medium of knit the untouchable heroes literally become tactile. Hanging limply from hangers, these supersuits evoke a sense of history and shared experience. The empty suits offer the space for us to imagine ourselves wearing the costume and call into question our essential fragility and vulnerability as pitted against the notion of super-being. Newport virtually ridicules the need for men to remain masculine, or live up to the rule of masculinity projected onto us in childhood, reiterating the idea of a disguise that we all wear to protect our softer selves from the world around us.

~~~~~~

1. From the artist's statement, submitted to the author in November 2007.

Matthew Barney, CREMASTER 3, 2002.
Production still, © 2002 Matthew Barney. Image courtesy of Gladstone Gallery. Photo: Chris Winget.

Matthew Barney

Matthew Barney was born in 1961 in San Francisco and brought up between Idaho and New York. A wrestler and footballer at high school, he enrolled at Yale to study medicine before transferring to study art. Graduating in 1989, he started creating work that combined sculptural installations with video, drawing inspiration from 1960s performance art and the work of Joseph Beuys, Marina Abramovic, Richard Serra and Bruce Nauman. He is best known for his *Cremaster* cycle, a series of five films created out of sequence between 1994 and 2002. In conjunction with his films, Barney produces drawings, photographs, sculptures and installations, which represent key aspects of each project's conceptual framework. His oeuvre thus entails film in combination with a diversity of other media and materials, united together to form a *gesamtkunstwerk* or total work of art.

~~~~~ From his earlier performances to his most recent cinematic endeavours, Barney has focused on an exploration of the body as a site of struggle, resistance and potential transformation. *Drawing Restraint*, a series of recorded performances and films spanning the entire career of the artist, examines the relationship between resistance and creativity through the creation of obstacles that attempt to turn drawing into a physical challenge. The tension between an imposed, fixed biological structure and a body in a constant state of mutation permeates his work: beings in a state of undifferentiation or pre-genital mode of experience—from androgynous fairies to genderless males and mutating character forms populate his universe.

~~~~~ Barney's interest in the body would naturally extend into a fascination with costume. As Barney gradually started incorporating narrative, cinematic

Matthew Barney

elements in his work, so did costume begin to occupy an all the more pivotal role in his practice; one just needs to contrast his earlier naked performances with the Rococo parade outfits, tantalising textures and exotic dresses of *Drawing Restraint 9*. Storytelling and cloth are inextricably woven together: costume acts as a catalyst in both character and narrative development. Thus in *Drawing Restraint 9* the two main characters dress in elaborate Japanese Shinto attire, complete with fur cloaks and shells attached to their backs; the extravagance and exoticism of the clothes adds an otherwordly quality to the way the characters move. Here costume acts as a signifier of the characters' difficulty in navigating through a foreign environment while simultaneously being suggestive of the tension between physical confinement and creativity, a tension at the core of the entire *Drawing Restraint* series. In *Cremaster 2* a similar theme is conveyed through *fin-de-siècle* fashion and the use of corseting in the opening sequence of the film where the three participants of the séance, including the male character, wear confining corsets that bind and restrict them.

~~~~~ Tools in the development of narrative, Barney's costumes have meta-narrative qualities that extend far beyond their alignment with cinematic form: grandiose and operatic, they often seem to exist independently of the films themselves and are charged with energies that make them appear somewhat larger than life. The persistent attention to elaborate, sensuous detail and their richly organised aesthetics lend them sitelessness suggestive of sculpture. However, these grand structures are also very much a part of Barney's creative

Matthew Barney, *CREMASTER 5*, 1997.
Production still, © 1997 Matthew Barney. Image courtesy of Gladstone Gallery. Photo: Michael James O'Brien.
OPPOSITE: Matthew Barney, *DRAWING RESTRAINT 9*, 2005.
Production still, © 2005 Matthew Barney. Image courtesy of Gladstone Gallery, New York. Photo: Chris Winget.

machinery, they are as responsible for narrative and plot development as any other element of his film work. Indeed, oftentimes a change in a character's disposition or nature is symbolised by a change in costume, literally playing out the story of the film on the very body of Barney's characters.

Barney's large-scale three-dimensional work combines and mutates familiar objects into new amalgamations; likewise the costumes challenge conventional notions of dress by combining organic with industrial materials such as teflon, filters from air conditioners and thermoplastic materials. Hybrid and mutated sculptural objects, they sit comfortably within Barney's universe of fluid energies and polymorphous transformations.

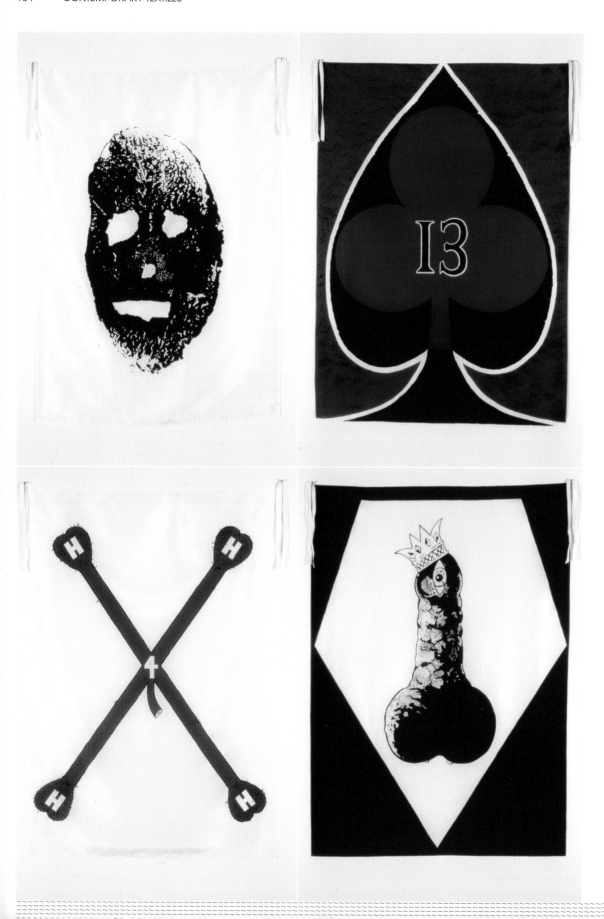

Mike Kelley

One of the most influential artists of his generation, Mike Kelley was born in Wayne, Detroit and lives and works in Los Angeles. In the early 1970s Kelley attended the University of Michigan in Ann Arbor and together with Jim Shaw, Niagara and Cary Loren founded Destroy All Monsters, an art-rock music band influenced by Sun Ra, Futurist noise, the Velvet Underground and Dadaist Bruitism. The band adopted a confrontational approach to traditional rock, incorporating instruments such as cheap keyboards, broken electronic devices, vacuum cleaners and hot-wired toys. Kelley left the band in the summer of 1976 to attend CAL Arts in Los Angeles and began a series of projects using a variety of creative methods, including performance, writing, painting and sculpture. He started to gain recognition outside Los Angeles in the mid-1980s, and has since exhibited widely in group and solo shows, including invitations to show at Documenta and the Venice Biennale.

~~~~~ Kelley's practice has ranged from ritualistic performances and multi-room installations to collaborations with artists such as Tony Oursler and Paul McCarthy. Throughout the early 1980s he performed a series of pieces that evoked themes alive in the American imaginary, including notions of the dysfunctional, the juvenile and the psychosexual. In 1986, he performed his well-known *Plato's Cave, Rothko's Chapel, Lincoln's Profile* at the Massachusetts Institute of Technology with a live accompaniment by the band Sonic Youth. He subsequently decided to end his work in performance and in the late 1980s and turned his creative method to textile-based sculpture. Kelley's recent work has him creating

Mike Kelley, *Horse Dancers*, 2005.
Mixed media, 76.2 x 137.2 x 78.7 cm. Image courtesy of the artist and Gagosian Gallery. Photo: Fredrik Nilsen.

Mike Kelley

a series of fascinatingly grotesque sculptural objects, fashioned from filthy, worn
-out stuffed animals the artist found in thrift stores. Kelley's creative method
evidences his fascination with the nostalgic, a self-consciousness couched in a
shared western history of childhood mediated by political and moral critique.
~~~~ There is a fundamental tension in Kelley's work, where the viewer is
never quite sure if the works displayed are an earnest elaboration of childhood
detritus to some defined conceptual end, or a tongue-in-cheek critique of the
worst kind of autobiographical artistic practice. It is perhaps safe to say that
there is evidence of both drives in Kelley's creative approach, and the ambiguity
inherent in his work only serves to deepen the widespread fascination with his
recent sculptural efforts.

Mike Kelley, *Snakeskin Studloaf*, 2005.
Mixed media, 30.5 x 114.3 x 35.6 cm. Image courtesy of the artist and Gagosian Gallery. Photo: Fredrik Nilsen.

Nick Cave, *Soundsuit*, 2005.
Cotton knits, fabricated appliqué surface, metal armature and found vintage metal flowers.

Nick Cave, *Soundsuit*, 2005.
Cotton knits, found appliqué stitched kitty-cat face mask, appliqué embellished surface, found porcine bird figurines and metal armature.

Nick Cave

In his *Soundsuits* series, Nick Cave fashions a stage where the theatre of racial politics, cultural identity and psychological self-representation play out in epic proportions. His sculptural costumes are not only made from a vast array of materials and techniques, but they represent a considerable range of issues that pre-occupy the collective imagination.

~~~~ The sheer scale of many of the pieces in the *Soundsuits* series is impressive, often over life-sized, these structures can be worn on the body in performance, or placed in a gallery space as static objects, offering multiple points of entry for the viewer to engage with the work. Cave builds his suits from a collection of found and manufactured objects, including fabrics, beads, sequins, bottle caps, old toys, twigs and hair. By virtue of their construction,

Cave's *Soundsuits* often make a noise when they are worn in performance, creating an eerie soundtrack to the otherwordly imagery they create. The resulting scenes, whether static or dynamic, are physically and conceptually intricate, weaving a rich narrative of cultural signifiers to suggest various conflicts and relationships.

~~~~~ Cave's *Soundsuits* are suggestive of African ceremonial costumes, used by many cultures to evoke certain powers, or remind the community of shared histories and myths. The same principles run through Cave's work, where he uses elements from a variety of cultures to create something like a shared ceremonial tool with which we can begin to dream a cross-cultural myth or history that accounts for both what unites and divides international community.

Paddy Hartley, *Spreckley 2 (multiple view)*, 2007.
Officer's uniform, digital embroidery, Lazertran inkjet print. Photo: Paddy Hartley, Project Facade.

Paddy Hartley

Trained in ceramics and sculpture, British artist Paddy Hartley explores the space between art and science in his creative approach. He has been involved in projects examining the origins of facial reconstruction, and the way religious organisations have been manipulating attitudes towards medical technologies since the advent of anything like a medical institution.

~~~~~ *A Project Facade* takes his research into these cross-disciplinary areas a step further. Paying homage to the cosmetic surgery of Sir Harold Gillies and his unrivalled ability to push the parameters of the profession beyond all known techniques during and in the aftermath of the First World War, the project is a collaborative effort between Hartley, biomaterial scientist Ian Thompson and the Gillies archive curator Andrew Bamji. Its primary aim is to narrate the stories and experiences of individuals who were facially disfigured during armed conflict. Hartley reconstructs military uniforms, onto which he embroiders scraps of information relating to the person who might have worn it in battle. "The uniform sculptures and accompanying face garments pool all the information I have from a variety of sources to present a collage of experience of that individual. Faces are left blank, pointing to the horror of a face literally effaced by war."[1] These arresting structures literally embody the physical and emotional cost of war, with Hartley recreating the ghostly forms of the victims of war that were literally defaced through their commitments to duty.

1. Taken from the artist's statement, submitted to the author in October 2007.

CLOCKWISE TOP TO BOTTOM: Paddy Hartley, *Spreckley 1 (pocket detail)*, 2007. Officer's uniform, digital embroidery, Lazertran inkjet print. Photo: Paddy Hartley, Project Facade.

Paddy Hartley, *Spreckley 2 (pocket detail)*, 2007. Officer's uniform, digital embroidery, Lazertran inkjet print, vintage lace. Photo: Paddy Hartley, Project Facade.

Paddy Hartley, *Spreckley 2 (pocket detail)*, 2007. Officer's uniform, digital embroidery, Lazertran inkjet print. Photo: Paddy Hartley, Project Facade.

Paddy Hartley, *Spreckley 1 (sleeve detail)*, 2007. Officer's uniform, digital embroidery, vintage lace. Photo: Paddy Hartley, Project Facade.

Paddy Hartley, *Spreckley 2 (Surgical notes chest detail)*, 2007. Officer's uniform, digital embroidery, Lazertran inkjet print. Photo: Paddy Hartley, Project Facade.

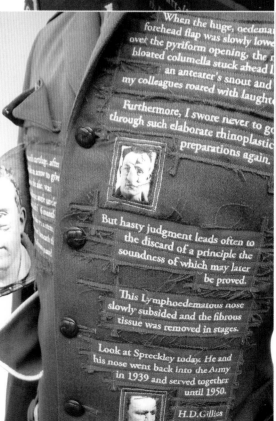

Magdalena Abakanowicz, *Seated Figures*, 1974–1979. 18 burlap and resin figures, each approximately 104 x 51 x 66 cm, steel stands, each one 76 x 46 x 22 cm. Collection Virginia Museum of Fine Arts. Photo: Jan Kosmowski.

Magdalena Abakanowicz

Born in Falenty, Poland in 1930, Magdalena Abakanowicz' work was first brought to international prominence when she won the Grand Prize at the 1965 São Paulo Biennial. Aged nine at the time of the Nazi-Soviet invasion of Poland, Abakanowicz completed her fine art university education during some of the strictest years of imposed Socialist Realism. However it is also during this period that she took instruction in weaving and fibre design. Coinciding with the gradual liberalisation of art in Poland, the 1960s saw Abakanowicz largely abandon the watercolours and gouaches of her early works in favour of large-scale fabric sculptures that confirmed her success as a fine artist. These *Abakans* (named after herself) combined distinctly hand-crafted fabrics with monumental sculpture: untwining and then dying strands of sisal rope collected from dockyards, reweaving them to create great cocoon-like structures that were to be hung from the ceiling in series.

~~~~~ *Black Environment*—15 suspended *Abakans* barely skimming the floor—transforms woven sisal into the experiential potential of an interactive environment: allowing the viewer to enter them through openings, each hanging piece offers the possibility of an intimate relationship or a unique experience. Upon entering Abakanowicz' pieces, the viewer is given a second skin to inhabit, an interior space that brings the non-visual—darkness, texture and isolation—to the fore. These ropes no longer bind; instead they provide a resting place or shelter, that is perhaps inconsistent with the authoritarian manner in which they command the space of their exhibition.

Magdalena Abakanowicz, *80 Backs*, 1976–1980. Burlap and resin, 66 x 50 x 60 cm. Installation view near Calgary, 1982. Photo: Dirk Bakker.

~~~~~~~ Since the 1970s, the focus of Abakanowicz' practice has been the creation of series of figurative, largely human, sculptures in burlap cloth that variously take the form of masses of headless standing bodies, seated torsos, featureless heads and hybrid beasts. Perhaps echoing her personal experience of the Soviet Communist regime, her *Crowds* series constitute a vast population of anonymous but emphatically individual adult-sized figures who stand resolute, always facing the same direction. Here the imposed collectivism and commonality of a political past conflicts with the refusal of the figures to conform to a perfect vision of repeatability: hand-cast and individually formed, each of these apparent 'everymen' retains a dignity and a resistance in their singularity, a fact underscored by their invitation to the viewer to walk between

them, to contemplate them one by one. The use of woven hessian, evoking not only the artist's canvas and the utilitarian values of cloth sacking but also the corporeal self-mortification of the hairshirt, signifies both a punishing repentance for terrible sins and an endurance that makes the status of Abakanowicz' figures even more opaque. Symbolising both the nameless figures of the 'masses' and the reality of the individual, Abakanowicz' works reach much further than the socio-political histories of oppressed peoples to confront their viewer with the instabilities of the human condition and the true mysteries of civilisation. Whether ready to march or silently waiting in line, they simultaneously evoke the fear of the crowd and the uncanniness of the void, the duality and interrelatedness of oppression and liberation.

SP

PACES

Christo and Jeanne-Claude

Christo and Jeanne-Claude have been creating environmental installations for over four decades. They have covered, draped and folded fabric over, through and around found objects, natural landscapes and constructed forms. Their practice has challenged traditional definitions of sculpture and architecture while creating a discourse for themes such as the ephemeral, the impermanent and the environmental. Echoes of constructivism, happenings, land art and the tradition of the draped figure—as epitomised in Rodin's sculptures—are all counted among their influences.

~~~~~ Since 1961, and the installation of their first monumental projects *Dockside Packages* in Cologne and *Rideau de Fer*, Paris, 1962, the artists have executed various large-scale projects, all of which have enjoyed iconic status within contemporary art: *Wrapped Coast*, 1969, a covering of cliff-lined shore area with one million square feet of erosion-control synthetic mesh fabric; *Valley Curtain*, 1970–1972, a bright 400 metre long curtain suspended between two mountains; *Surrounded Islands*, 1980–1983, more than six million square feet of pink polypropylene fabric floating around eleven islands; *The Umbrellas, Japan-USA*, 1984–1991, a simultaneous installation of thousands of umbrellas in the Ibaraki Prefecture, Japan and Tejon Pass, California. But of all their projects, *Wrapped Reichstag*, Berlin, 1971–1995, is perhaps the most ambitious and challenging of their entire career. "The only place in the world" Christo explains "where east and west were meeting, with tremendous drama and space in an extraordinary situation was Berlin. The only structure that was under the jurisdiction of the Americans, the Soviets, the English, the French, and the two Germanys

was the Reichstag. No other structure was under the jurisdiction of all the allied forces. This is how the Reichstag project originated in the early 1970s". The project has a long history of setbacks, being turned down by officials three times and finally coming to fruition in 1995, after 25 years of effort. It encapsulates almost all of the themes that the duo have explored throughout their artistic partnership: the choice of a site with a potent symbolic value and a long, intricate history; disruption of the surrounding space; the opposition between the hidden, the covered and the exposed; and the transformation of known forms into uncanny, ghostly presences.

~~~~~ The significance of their work lies not only in the selection of key historical buildings, such as the Reichstag and the Pont-Neuf, but also in their difficult negotiations with authorities, landowners, banks, planners, community groups

and political parties. Years and sometimes decades are spent and at times projects are abandoned altogether as a result of complications in the planning stages. This laborious process is documented in a variety of media—preparatory drawings, books, films and videos, and in documentaries about each specific project. The works highlight process and evoke issues relating to ownership and control of public space: space that is lived and experienced on an everyday basis. What separates Christo and Jeanne-Claude from some other Land or Environmental artists of their generation is this consistency in choosing sites that people relate to, sites that are integral to everyday life: an approach that necessitates a rejection of both isolated areas and the self enclosed space of the institution. Through their insistence on constantly exposing the mechanisms behind each

Christo and Jeanne-Claude, *Wrapped Trees*, 1997–1998.
Fondation Beyeler and Berower Park, Riehen, Switzerland.

Christo and Jeanne-Claude

project's conception, production and installation, they reveal the spatial as the locus of power and conflict. "What space signifies is do's and don'ts —"Henri Lefebvre wrote "and this brings us back to power. Space lays down the law because it implies a certain order—and hence also a certain disorder. Space commands bodies. This is its raison d'être". Christo and Jeanne-Claude take the fully owned and regulated space of urban planning, introduce disturbances and interruptions and transform it into a utopian spectacle. They work in total freedom, accepting no sponsorship for any of the projects and financing everything themselves.

At the core of their work lies an attempt to break with the cult of personalised, transcendental expression through the staging of works that, though monumental, remain impermanent and ephemeral. Their temporary works survive only through preparatory photographs, films and books; they are most often dismantled days or weeks after they are erected. The projects incorporate a variety of materials including ropes, steel and aluminum but the most important material is fabric. Fragile and delicate, cloth encapsulates the vulnerability, temporariness and fragility of their work.

1. Mantegna, Gianfranco, "Interview with Christo and Jeanne-Claude", *Journal of Contemporary Art*.
2. Lefebvre, Henri, *The Production of Space*, London: Wiley-Blackwell, 1991.

Craig Fisher

Craig Fisher aspires to create something like an iconography of multiple popular references, all of which need to unpicked to fully appreciate their place in his site-specific narrative. Familiar objects, confused by Fisher's representational interplay, produce a nearly nightmarish scene of soft-edged, yet aggressive, symbolism. This is emphasised by the alternative places he chooses to show his work; as part of the *Trick Peaser* show, in the specialist travel goods Mandarina Duck Flagship Store, and a Beckett Boxing Gym in London. Fisher uses these locales to play off his sculptural pieces against an environment rich with signifiers, heightening the impact of his installation work.

~~~~~ Fisher has exhibited as part of a Crafts Council exhibition entitled *Boys Who Sew* in 2004, his work is led by a fascination with stitch and the connotation that it often holds. He carefully selects fabric to accentuate his conceptual ambitions, displacing the feminine character of the material with masculine subject matter, all hand-embroidered with a delicate decorative stitch.

~~~~~ By depicting subjects and scenes of violence with soft fabrics associated with the domestic, Fisher successfully subverts the masculine content of his work. Fisher's work has an essential duality that makes it utterly engaging, recreating everything from soldiers and astronauts to piles of vomit and urine stains, all fashioned from beautiful fabrics and adorned with delicate haberdashery.

~~~~~ Fisher works with his concept of 'the space in between', the seductive ambiguity where the real and the image meet as an unidentifiable thing, discipline, state or position. As viewers, this challenges our perceived difference between

Craig Fisher, *Leak*, 2005.
Car upholstery fabric and mixed media, dimensions variable.
OPPOSITE: Craig Fisher, *Get Rid*, 2006.
Felt, neoprene, sequins, embroidery cotton, styrofoam, card and wood.

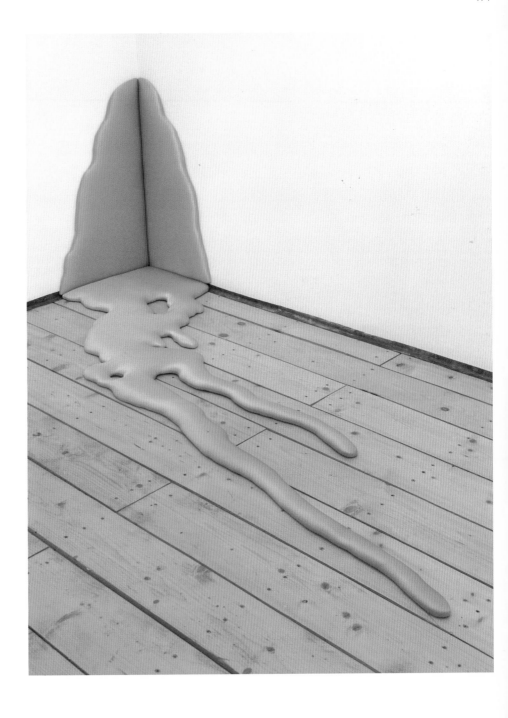

the object and our engagement with it in the artist's context. Fisher plays with scale and meaning, throwing up our expectations of science, sewing, couture, sculpture and craft. He presents technology as a plaything, children's toys in adult sizes, adorning undesirable objects in seductive materials, such as his upholstering of bombs in Chinese silk, so that they appear exotic, stylish and desirable. However, we are not comfortable in Fisher's soft world of hard things, there is something unnerving, things are not as they might seem. Though his mutations appear to be benign, they still problematise our accepted categories and are therefore potentially dangerous or unsettling.

~~~~ Fisher is currently working on large scale sculptural installations using various fabrics that question representations of violence, disaster and macho stereotypes. He is particularly interested in playing with boundaries, mixing techniques of art and craft, referencing both 'high' and 'low' culture and exposing everyday narratives that sit between reality and fantasy. Fisher explores boundaries as potential spaces of slippage, of accidents, which allow for discoveries beyond confined and referenced fields of art production. Fisher challenges our habits of looking by presenting work encouraging us to perceive this essential 'state in between' in which much of his artistic practice resides.

Freddie Robins

Freddie Robins' work is about perfection. A constant battle against the imperfections, failings and roughness of the material world drives her creative approach, choosing to work in knit to embody underlying values of good craftsmanship and attention to detail. Despite her theoretical commitments, Robins acknowledges that true perfection is totally unachievable, serving as a guide rather than a goal.

~~~~~ Robin's uses the Shima Seiki WholeGarment® in her artistic practice, a computerised, V-bed flat machine, capable of knitting a seamless three-dimensional garment in one process, which Robins employs to make whole life-sized human bodies. She configures her multi-formed inflated figures to interact physically and emotionally, effecting strange lifeless energies that explore deformity, uniformity, anonymity and conformity.

~~~~~ In *The Perfect*, organ-less, spineless knitted skins lie discarded on the gallery floor as in the aftermath of a human tragedy, a battlefield after the slaughter, or perhaps the embodied failing in the quest for perfection. Issues surrounding domesticity, subverting preconceptions, and disrupting the medium from the passive, all play a role in Robins work. She takes up various visual signifiers to blur the boundaries between craft and art, indeed Robins directly questions the negative associations with the word 'craft' with her piece *Craft Kills*, a hanging life-sized grey figure, stabbed through the legs and chest with knitting needles, which also cascade around the figure on the floor, the words 'craft kills' emblazoned across its chest. Here Robins takes up a common debate in textile art, ripped through the very body of her fascinating, at times otherworldly, work.

Freddie Robins, *Craft Kills*, 2002.
Machine knitted wool, knitting needles, 200 x 68 x 38 cm. Installed at firstsite at the Minories Art Gallery, Colchester. Photo: Douglas Atfield.
OPPOSITE: Freddie Robins, *Anyway*, 2002.
Machine knitted wool, 165 x 300 x 300 cm. Installed at firstsite at the Minories Art Gallery, Colchester. In the collection of the Castle Museum, Nottingham. Photo: Douglas Atfield.

OPPOSITE: Seamus McGuinness, 21g, dimensions variable.
Photo: Marcus Couinhan.

Laura Viskerson, Offering, 2000.
Église St.-Roch. Photo: Pierre Soulard.

Laura Vickerson

Laura Vickerson is interested in the 'stuff' of life, that is, the materiality of our lived experience. Her large-scale installation pieces often include discarded objects and materials, which were valued in a previous life but for some reason have become obsolete or undesirable. Vickerson takes the detritus of everyday life and reinvigorates it, adding meaning and value through composition and place.
~~~~~ Vickerson often uses decaying flowers as raw materials for her installations, pinning material to the wall with a nearly obsessive application. Her method effects metres of velvety-looking organic fabric, reaching from floor to ceiling, across whole rooms, in a dramatic display of themes of mortality, fertility and femininity. These thick, gushing, deep red swathes of fabric appear like gigantic rivers of blood that collect in pools within the installation space.

~~~~~ Rose petals symbolise love, and the thorny rose, pain and pleasure, this is also reflective of a life cycle that Vickerson explores in her work, which in turn reminds us of our own mortality and the pain of love and loss, the act of physically or emotionally bleeding dry. Relationships with the material world and with each other are at the centre of Vickerson's creative approach. She uses the metaphor of the curtain to reference this threshold between the interior and exterior, nature and nurture, this world and the next. With her emotional, nearly spiritual, work, Vickerson appeals to all that is common and divine in the human experience.

Seamus McGuinness

Seamus McGuinness' work uses the metaphor of clothing to investigate themes of life and death, His work specifically concerns the increasing suicide rates among young Irish males between the years of 2003 and 2006. *Lost Portraits— Materialising Stories* involves the engagement of a hundred young people who lost their lives to suicide, and the impact these tragedies have had on families and communities.

~~~~~ McGuinness' research revealed that bereaved families and friends of suicide victims did not know how to emotionally deal with the deceased's clothing. In one case, a mother revealed she carefully laundered some of the items, as if to be worn again by her son, whilst others she put in a plastic bag to preserve his smell on the material. McGuiness' pieces are ephemeral,

spiritual and deal with these themes of absence and presence. *21 Grams,* for example, relates to the reportedly instant amount of weight lost by the body at the moment of death. *100 Lived Lives,* consists of 92 white shirt collars, themselves weighing 21 grams each. His pieces look unfinished or unravelled, collars with no shirt, suspended in mid-air with loose threads creating a ghostly scene, like the body torn form the soul, an unfinished young life reduced to scraps of memory. McGuiness' work is as much about the effect of suicide on the living as representing the absence of who is gone. Cloth is our second skin; it is physically and metaphorically like our own bodies, with the potential to be injured, degraded or marked. McGuinnes uses this metaphor to great effect in his highly emotional installations.

OPPOSITE: Mary Tuma, *Homes for the Disembodied*. Chiffon, thread, wire, 365 x 731 x 152 cm. Made in Palestine Collection. Photo: Station Museum, Houston, TX.

Mary Tuma, *Internal Power*. Crochet installation, ribbon, hemp, thread, stones, cave, 335 x 1219 x 609 cm. Collection of Naim Farhat. Photo: Anton Stephan.

Mary Tuma

Mary Tuma was born in Oakland, California, but her Palestinian origins feature large in her work. Since the early 1990s, she has been creating works that speak of exile, memory, the body and diaspora. Her artistic practice combines costume design, textiles and found or discarded objects in installations which are subtle and introverted, yet confront issues of violence, death, and the misfortunes of the Palestinian people.

~~~~~ *Homes for the Disembodied*, originally created and shown in Jerusalem during 2000 and later included in the seminal *Made in Palestine* exhibition, is a memorial to the 300,000 Palestinians who fled from the West Bank and Gaza after the 1967 Israeli occupation of east Jerusalem. Tuma has sewn 50 yards of black chiffon to create five continuous dresses recreated according to a traditional Palestinian pattern. Placed in line and hung from wire forms at the necks and shoulders, the dresses are of monumental dimensions but the lightness and delicacy of their material creates forms vulnerable to the space in which they are displayed. The interconnectedness of the work suggests the collective adversity faced by the Palestinian people. Tuma describes the heroic scale of the dresses as a powerful metaphor for "the strength and courage of Palestinian women who must carry on in unjust circumstances they have little power to change". A meditation on loss, mourning and remembrance *Homes for the Disembodied* functions as an invitation for the displaced and the uprooted. "It is very much a spirit dwelling place", Tuma explains, " a comfort zone for spirits without a home".[1]

Passages refers to another moment in Palestinian history: the Al Aqsa Intifada, the second major wave of violence between the Israelis and the Palestinians. Cradle, or ship-like structures hang from the ceiling and walls, covered with commercial clothing patterns suggesting the objectification of the 'other' in media coverage of the Palestinian/Israeli conflict, they act like passages that document the circumstances of individual deaths. Tuma calls attention to the hollow representations of political conflict, through the flattening of bodies that remain faceless. Themes of the body reappear in Tuma's more personal, introspective work. Internal Systems, composed of crocheted nervous systems and organs that hang and float free in space, explores the effects of the emotions on the body's interior and was produced after a turbulent physical and emotional period in Tuma's life, while Dancing Girls an ascendance of tricycles dressed in lace, net and ribbon, examines the transformation that the body goes through with change and death. Her work evokes various physical, emotional and political transformations and conflicts, underlining narratives of displacement and alienation on both a personal and national scale. Through her work, Tuma deploys powerful metaphors for the human condition, and how the characteristics of our cultural or political identities often gets played out on the materiality of the body or the landscape.

1. Taken from the artist's statement, submitted to the author in October 2007.

OPPOSITE RIGHT: Susie MacMurray, *Shell* (detail), 2006.
Shells, velvet, dimensions variable, installed at Pallant House Gallery.

OPPOSITE LEFT: Susie MacMurray, *Echo* (detail), 2006.
Dimensions variable. York St Mary's, York Museums Trust.

Susie MacMurray, *Echo*, 2006.
Dimensions variable. York St Mary's, York Museums Trust.

Susie MacMurray

From a background in orchestral music, Susie MacMurray now deploys the visual language of repetition characteristic of her formal training toward fulfiling the ambitions of her textile practice. MacMurray moved towards making, because she wanted to get her hands on 'stuff', the stuff of textiles, the medium that now provides her with a visual analogy for the musical language she once employed. She collects materials, some of which might lie around in her studio space for some time, until the right context presents itself so she can reinvent them to take on another life.

~~~~~ MacMurray wants to share her instinctive response to material, for us to enjoy the primary emotion of our 'encounter' with the work. She favours the qualities and contradictions of natural materials, their tenuous existence and finitude akin to our own mortality, Both the frightening and wonderful, the fragile and beautiful, inhabit the haunting scenes characteristic of MacMurray's work.

~~~~~ MacMurray's *Shell* piece was embedded in the stairwell and entrance space within Pallant House in Chichester, a Grade 1 listed Queen Anne townhouse dating from 1712. From July 2006–April 2007, MacMurray's *Shell* is a deeply rich embellishment of the internal walls, ordered rows of over 20,000 empty muscle shells filled with crimson red silk velvet tongues run from floor to ceiling. The combination of man-made voluptuous velvet and the natural skeleton of the dead shell, merged together to form a fetish of the organic and the ornamental, each coveted death side by side in an ordered graveyard of arrested love and fabricated desire.

~~~~~ Two essential elements make up the founding principles of MacMurray's work, her pieces are simultaneously wide-reaching and meticulous in detail, tactile in quality and fragile in nature.

~~~~~ MacMurray makes the intangibility of music tangible, her installations fill rooms just as the sound of her melodies might once have, with each piece of the installation participating in a grand orchestral of the visual. In *Echoes,* MacMurray creates something like a mute violin piece, where nearly 10,000 barely visible hairnets fill an entire minster. The hairnets themselves are fashioned from the discarded hairs of over 3,500 violin bows, made from horse tail hair in a grand gesture of renewal and reconceptualisation characteristic of the artist's work. MacMurray has worked with feathers, shells, hair, latex, cotton earplugs and plastic food wrap, carefully assessing the characteristics of each material she deploys to seek the emotional pitch necessary to activate its internal voice.

Jennifer Angus, detail of *Grammar of Ornament at the Madison Museum of Contemporary Art*, 2007. Hand-printed wallpaper, circular frame with digital print and insects, and Tosena Albata (black cicadas). Photo: Tyler Robbins.

Jennifer Angus

Canadian artist Jennifer Angus creates large scale installations featuring exotic petrified insects of the most astonishing shapes and colours—moths, beetles, grasshoppers and weevils. The insects are arranged into intricate geometric patterns inspired by Japanese, Indian, Egyptian and floral textile designs. The exquisite attention to pattern has made her a pioneer of contemporary textile art. Angus combines her love of pattern with elements drawn from Victorian science, entomology and cultural anthropology.

~~~~~ *A Terrible Beauty,* her 2006 installation at the Textile Museum of Canada, is a marvellous take on the human impulse to contain and command nature. Split into three different rooms, with each space representing a chapter in the story of an imaginary Victorian insect collector, *A Terrible Beauty* reflects upon themes such as adventure, travel, storytelling and the compulsion to collect and preserve the natural world. Angus creates her own fascinating *wunderkammers* reminiscent of those compiled by colonial explorers, etching Victorian poems on the backs of metallic beetles and creating shadow boxes with insect samplers spelling out nursery rhymes. The viewer is at once seduced into a familiarity with common patterns and shapes, and jolted out of that comfort when the material comprising those patterns becomes obvious. Like elsewhere in her work, Angus places the viewer in both a physical and psychological maze, amidst a world of science, fiction and fantasy.

Jennifer Angus, detail of *Grammar of Ornament* at the Madison Museum of Contemporary Art, 2007.
Hand-printed wallpaper, circular frame with digital print and insects, and Tosena Albata (black cicadas). Photo: Tyler Robbins.

Yinka Shonibare, *The Crowning*, 2007
Two mannequins, Dutch, Wax printed cotton textile, shoes, coir matting, artificial silk flowers, 160 x 280 x 210cm

Yinka Shonibare

Born in London and raised largely in the cultural melting pot that is Lagos, Nigeria, Yinka Shonibare is acutely aware of the meaning of multiculturalism. The artist's preoccupation with the idea of rich, historical and cultural tapestries is apparent in the sensorial excitement of his work. By forcing unlikely elements together into surprising and humourous combinations, Shonibare exposes the myth of cultural authenticity to reveal the true complexity of cultural identities and the many conflicting stories behind their origin.

~~~~~ His ethos is especially well materialised in the bold and colourful batik fabrics he often uses. Seen today as representative of the African identity, these fabrics were originally appropriated from Indonesia by Dutch colonists and later imported to Africa from Manchester. Shonibare says "it's the fallacy of that

Yinka Shonibare, *The Swing (After Fragonard)*, 2001. Dutch wax printed cotton textile, life-sized mannequin, swing, artificial foliage. © Tate. Purchased 2002. Image courtesy the artist and Stephen Friedman Gallery, London.

signification that I like. It's the way I view culture—it's an artificial construct."[1] He stretches the fabrics onto canvases or has them made into Victorian dresses for headless mannequins with which he re-stages scenes from western art history. This theatrical and playful aesthetic is a reaction against traditional rules that have governed the exhibition of art, taking cues from the American civil rights and feminist movements of the 1950s and 60s. Shonibare realised early on that he could take the token elements used to define and limit his cultural identity and turn them in on themselves, creating the potential for a new, more accurate representation of the different perspectives from which a cultural identity is formed and stabilised. As Shonibare observes "I could challenge my relationship to authority with humour and parody in mimicking and mirroring".[2]

~~~~~ In his installation work, Shonibare often covers shoes, upholstery and bowls with these 'Africanised' fabrics, setting them in a typically European context borrowed from the cultural history of the western world. Shonibare often creates energetic installations with headless figures adorned in traditional western dress made out of these purportedly African Dutch-wax fabrics, drawing you into a theatre of cultural signifiers bashing up against one another. In so doing, Shonibare blurs the distinction between the two cultures and underlines the way they invent one another through fantasy and misinformation.

~~~~~ In his *How to Blow up Two Heads at Once (Gentlemen)*, Shonibare creates two headless mannequins dressed in gentlemen's clothing, pointing duelling pistols at the space where one another's head should be. On the far

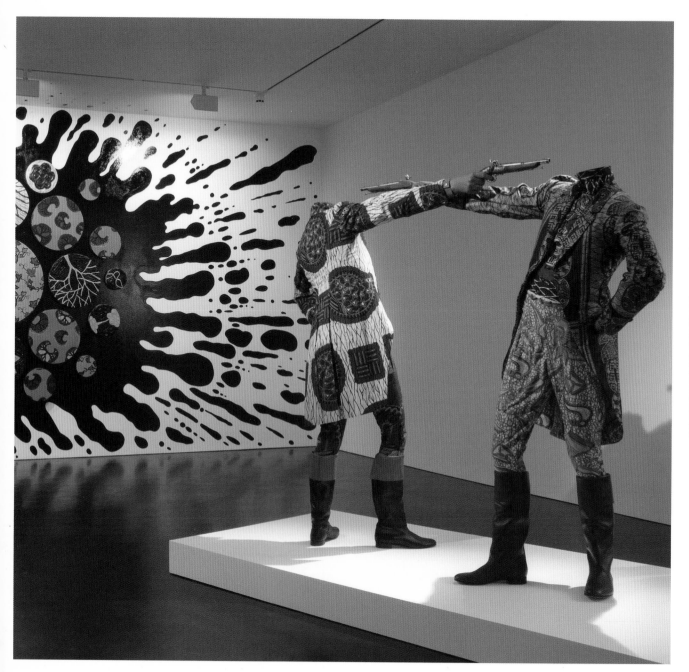

Yinka Shonibare, *How to Blow up Two Heads at Once (Gentlemen),* 2006. Two mannequins, two guns, Dutch, wax printed cotton textile, leather riding boots, plinth 175 x 245 x 122 cm.

Yinka Shonibare

wall behind the two figures there is an explosion of colour, swirling patterns suggestive of something like a cheerful blood splatter. Shonibare's use of costume is key to the concept of his work, in form and shape the mannequins wear clothing traditionally associated with western civilisation, but the fabric from which those costumes are made are associated with a constructed view of African culture, forcing an uncomfortable marriage between the two concepts of self and nationhood. The energy of the resulting installation poses all manner of questions about the ontological relationship between seemingly distinct cultural identities, highlighting how viscous result can come from our incomplete attempts at understanding and defining others, and indeed, ourselves.

1. Taken from the artist's interview with Pernilla Holmes in *ART News Online,* October 2002.
2. Taken from the artist's interview with Pernilla Holmes in *ART News Online,* October 2002.

Yinka Shonibare, *Mr and Mrs Andrews Without Their Heads*, 1998
Wax-print cotton costumes on armatures, dog, mannequin, bench, gun, 165 x 570 x 254 cm.

DRAWINGS

Andrea Dezsö
b. 1968, Transylvania (Hungary); lives in New York (America)
~~~~~ Selected Exhibitions: 2007 *Pricked: Extreme Embroidery* (group exh.), Museum of Arts and Design, New York ~~2006 *Andrea Dezsö: My Country* (solo exh.), Hungarian Cultural Center, New York

Annie Whiles
b. 1967, Nottingham (Britain); lives in London (Britain)
~~~~~ Selected Exhibitions: 2007 *Cuckoo* (solo exh.), Danielle Arnaud Gallery, London ~~2005 *Cloud and Vision* (group exh.), Museum of Garden History, London

Jessica Rankin
b. 1971, Sydney (Australia); lives in New York (America)
~~~~~ Selected Exhibitions: 2007 *Jessica Rankin* (solo exh.), White Cube, London ~~2005 *Mental Maps* (group exh.), Dorsky Curatorial Program, New York, NY ~~2004 *The Pale Cast of Thought* (solo exh.), The Project, New York

Karen Reimer
b. 1958; lives in Chicago (America)
~~~~~ Selected Exhibitions: 2006 *New Embroidery: Not Your Grandma's Doily* (group exh.), Contemporary Craft Museum, Portland ~~2004 *Boundary Troubles* (solo exh.), Monique Meloche Gallery, Chicago

Lisa Solomon
b. 1973, Tucson (America); lives in Tucson (America)
~~~~~ Selected Exhibitions: 2008 *Stretching the Threads* (group exh.), Atlantic Center for the Arts, Florida ~~2007 *Over the River and Through the Woods* (solo exh.), Little Bird Gallery, Los Angeles

Rachel Coleman
b. 1968, Manchester (Britain); lives in Lancashire (Britain)
~~~~~ Selected Exhibitions: 2006 *Lustre Contemporary Craft Fair* (group exh.), Lakeside Arts Centre, Nottingham ~~2003 *Unusual Objects* (group exh.), Royal Exchange Craft Gallery, Manchester

Orly Cogan
b. 1971, Jaffa (Israel); lives in New York (America)
~~~~~ Selected Exhibitions: 2007 *The Wonder of You* (solo exh.), Steven Wolf Fine Arts, Contemporary SF California ~~2006 *Threads of Memory* (group exh.), Dorsky Gallery, New York

Satoru Aoyama
b. 1973, Tokyo (Japan); lives in London (Britain) and Tokyo (Japan)
~~~~~ Selected Exhibitions: 2007 *Ancient Pixels* (solo exh.), Chicago Cultural Centre, Chicago ~~2007 *Crowing in the Studio* (solo exh.), Mizuma Art Gallery, Tokyo

Bente Sætrang
b. 1946, Oslo (Norway); lives in Oslo (Norway)
~~~~~ Selected Exhibitions: 2004, *Retrospective,* National Museum of Arts, Architecture and Design, Oslo

Tucker Schwarz
b. 1972, Florida (America); lives in San Fransisco (America)
~~~~~ Selected Exhibitions: 2005 *I'm sure I'm shouting* (solo exh.), Gregory Lind Gallery, New York ~~2003 *Sewn Together* (group exh.), Gregory Lind Gallery, New York

Tilleke Schwarz
b. 1946, Winterswijk, (The Netherlands); lives in Pijnacker (The Netherlands)
~~~~~ Selected Exhibitions: 2008 *Fabric of Myth* (group exh.), Compton Verney Art Gallery, Warwickshire ~~2008 *Tilleke Schwarz* (solo exh.), Museum Rijswijk, Rijswijk

Sybille Hotz
b. 1968, Darmstadt (Germany); lives in Berlin (Germany)
~~~~~ Selected Exhibitions: 2007 *Pricked: Extreme Embroidery* (group exh.), Museum of Arts and Design, New York ~~2007 *Vanishing* (solo exh.), Deck-Gallery for Contemporary Art, Stuttgart

PAINTINGS

Steve MacDonald
b. 1972, Jacksonville, Florida (America); lives in San Francisco (America)
~~~~~ Selected Exhibitions: 2007 *Thread* (group exh.), Studio 411 Venice Beach

Berend Strik
b.1960, Nijmegen (The Netherlands); lives in Amsterdam (The Netherlands)
~~~~~ Selected Exhibitions: 2008 *Berend Strik* (solo exh.), Galerie Fons Welters, Amsterdam ~~2005 *Lascivious Fortification, Shadow and Light* (solo exh.), Jack Tilton Gallery, New York

Cosima Von Bonin
b. 1962, Mombasa (Kenya); lives in Cologne (Germany)
~~~~~ Selected Exhibitions: 2007 *documenta 12* (group exh.), Kassel, Germany ~~2007 *Roger & Out* (solo exh.), The Museum of Contemporary Art, Los Angeles ~~2006 *Relax, It's Only a Ghost* (solo exh.), Friedrich Petzel Gallery, New York

Devorah Sperber
b. 1961, Detroit (America); lives in New York (America)
~~~~~ Selected Exhibitions: 2008 *Interpretations: Devorah Sperber* (solo exh.), MASS MoCA, North Adams ~~2007 *The Eye of the Artist: The Work of Devorah Sperber* (solo exh.), Brooklyn Museum of Art, New York

Elaine Reichek
b. 1943, New York (America); lives in New York (America)
~~~~~ Selected Exhibitions: 2007 *Pattern Recognition* (solo exh.), Nicole Klagsbrun Gallery, New York ~~2006 *Glossed in Translation* (solo exh.), Shoshana Wayne Gallery, Los Angeles ~~2006 *Material Culture: The Fine Art of Textiles* (group exh.), Salt Lake Art Centre, Salt Lake City

Ghada Amer
b. 1963, Cairo (Egypt); lives in New York (America)
~~~~~ Selected Exhibitions: 2007 *Ghada Amer* (solo exh.), MACRO Museo d' Arte Contemporanea Roma, Rome ~~2006 *Ghada Amer— Breathe into Me* (solo exh.), Gagosian Gallery, New York ~~2000 *Whitney Biennial* (group exh.), New York

Gillian Cooper
b. 1970, Motherwell (Britain); lives in Balfron (Britain)
~~~~~ Selected Exhibitions: 2007 *The Cutting Edge* (group exh.), National Museum of Scotland

Monika Auch
b. 1955, Biebesheim (Germany); lives in Muiderberg (The Netherlands)
~~~~~ Selected Exhibitions: 2007 *International Textile Biennial* (group exh.), Kaunas, Lithuania

Janis Jefferies
b. 1952, London (Britain); lives in London (Britain)
~~~~~ Select Exhibitions: 2008 *Inspired Design—Creative Entrepreneurial Textiles* (group exh.), Centre for Craft, Creativity and Design, North Carolina ~~2001 *Selvedges* (solo exh.),

Kent Henricksen
b. 1974, New Haven (America); lives in New York (America)
~~~~~ Selected Exhibitions: 2007, *Kent Henricksen: Gales and Gasps*, c/o - Atle Gerhardsen, Berlin ~~2007, *Kent Henricksen: Divine Deviltries*, John Connelly Presents, New York

Lara Schnitger
b. 1969, Haarlem (The Netherlands); lives in Los Angeles (America) and Amsterdam (The Netherlands)
~~~~~ Selected Exhibitions: 2005 *My Other Car is a Broom* (solo exh.), Magasin 3, Stockholm ~~2005 *Blacks on Blondes* (solo exh.), Triple Candie, New York

Lia Cook
b. 1942, Ventura (America); lives in Berkeley (America)
~~~~~ Selected Exhibitions: 2006 *Re-Embodied* (solo exh.), Nancy Margolis Gallery, New York, NY ~~2004 *Binary Traces* (solo exh.), Mills College Art Museum, Oakland

Maria E Piñeres
b. 1967, Medellin (Colombia); lives in Los Angeles (America)
~~~~~ Selected Exhibitions: 2006 *Palindromes* (solo exh.), Walter Maciel Gallery, Los Angeles, CA ~~2005 *A Rogues' Gallery* (solo exh.), DCKT Contemporary, New York, NY

Nava Lubelski
b. 1968, New York (America); lives in New York (America)
~~~~~ Selected Exhibitions: 2007 *Imperfectionism* (solo exh.), LMAKprojects, Brooklyn, NY ~~2007 *Spilled Milk* (solo exh.), OHT Gallery, Boston, MA

Rosemarie Trockel
b. 1952, Schwerte (Germany); lives in Cologne (Germany)
~~~~~ Selected Exhibitions: 2008 *Keramiken und Kollagen* (solo exh.), Galerie Crone, Berlin ~~2006 *Make your Own Life: Artists in and out of Cologne* (group exh.), Institute of Contemporary Art / University of Pennsylvania, Philadelphia ~~2005 *Post-Menopause* (solo exh.), Museum Ludwig, Cologne ~~2000 Rosemarie Trockel: *Metamorphoses et Mutations* (solo exh.), Centre National d' Art et de Culture Pompidou, Paris

Silja Puranen
b. 1961, Elimäki (Finland); lives in Öljymäki (Finland)
~~~~~ Selected Exhibitions: 2007 Galleria Katariina (solo exh.), Helsinki ~~2006 *7th Finnish Textile Triennial* (group exh.), Amos Anderson Art Museum, Helsinki

Tracey Emin
b. 1963, London (Britain); lives in London (Britain)
~~~~~ Selected Exhibitions: 2006 *More Flow* (solo exh.), Galleria Lorcan O'Neill, Rome ~~2005 *I Can Feel Your Smile* (solo exh.), Lehmann Maupin, New York

Wendy Huhn
b. 1953, Phoenix (America); lives in Dexter (America)
~~~~~ Selected Exhibitions: 2007 *Craft in America* (group exh.), Museum of Contemporary Craft, Portland ~~2001 *Extraordinary Textiles* (solo exh.), Springfield Museum, Oregon

SCULPTURES

Annet Couwenberg
b. 1950, Rotterdam (The Netherlands); lives in Baltimore (America)
~~~~~ Selected Exhibitions: 2007 *Whispering Frills* (solo exh.), Villa Julie Gallery, Stevenson ~~2003 *Common Thread* (group exh.), Memphis College of Art, Memphis

Annette Messager
b. 1943, Berck-sur-Mer (France); lives in Paris (France)
~~~~~ Selected Exhibitions: 2007 *Annette Messager* (solo exh.), Centre National d' Art et de Culture Pompidou, Paris ~~2007 *Mystic Truths* (group exh.), Auckland Art Gallery, Auckland ~~2005 *Venice Biennale* (group exh.), Venice

Benji Whalen
b. 1968, New York (America); lives in San Francisco (America)
~~~~~ Selected Exhibitions: 2007 *Claustrotopia* (solo exh.), Mogadishni, Copenhagen ~~2007 *Pricked: Extreme Embroidery* (group exh.), Museum of Arts and Design, New York ~~2002 *Evol* (solo exh.), Clementine Gallery, New York

Guerra de la Paz
Alain Guerra: b. 1968, Havana (Cuba); lives in Miami (America) / Fernando de la Paz: b. 1955, Matanza (Cuba); lives in Miami (America)
~~~~~ Selected Exhibitions: 2008 *Green Zone* (solo exh.), Daneyal Mahmood Gallery, New York ~~2007 *Flower Children* (solo exh.), Carol Jazzaz Gallery, Miami

Gyöngy Laky
b. 1944, Budapest (Hungary); lives in San Francisco (America)
~~~~~ Selected Exhibitions: 2007 *Intersections* (solo exh.), Braunstein/Quay Gallery, San Francisco ~~2005 *Kaunas Art Biennial* (group exh.), Kaunas ~~2004 *Celebrating Nature* (group exh.), Craft and Folk Art Museum, Los Angeles

Janet Cooper
b. 1937, New York (America); lives in Sheffield (America)
~~~~~ Selected Exhibitions: 2006 *Global Warning* (group exh.), Meeting House Gallery, New Marlborough ~~2005 *Recollected/Re-invented: The Narrative Craft Object* (group exh.), Brookfield Craft Centre, Brookfield

Janet Echelman
b. 1966, Tampa (America); lives in Brookline, Massachusetts
~~~~~ Select Installations: 2005 *She Changes*, Waterfront Plaza, Porto and Matosinhos ~~2000 *Window Treatment with 16 Tails*, Florence Lynch Gallery, New York

Jann Haworth
b. 1942, Hollywood (America); lives in Sundance (America)
~~~~~ Selected Exhibitions: 2006 *Jann Haworth: Artist's Cut* (solo exh.), Mayor Gallery, London ~~2005 *British Pop* (group exh.), Museo del Bellas Arte de Bilbao, Bilbao ~~2004 *Art and the Sixties: This was Tomorrow* (group exh.), Tate Britain, London

Dave Cole
b. New Hampshire (America); lives in Providence (America)
~~~~~ Selected Exhibitions: 2007 *Boys Craft* (group exh.), Hiafa Museum of Art, Jerusalem ~~2005 *The Knitting Machine and other Work* (solo exh.), MASS MoCA, Carolina

Laura Ford
b. 1961, Cardiff (Wales); lives in London (England)
~~~~~ Selected Exhibitions: 2005 *Venice Biennale* (group exh.), Venice ~~2004 *Wreckers* (solo exh.), Houldsworth Gallery, London

Lucy + Jorge Orta
Lucy Orta: b. 1966, Birmingham (Britain); lives in Paris (France) / Jorge Orta: b. 1953, Rosario (Argentina); lives in Paris (France)
~~~~~ Select Exhibitions: 2007 *Lucy Orta—Nexus Architecture* (solo exh.), Tramway, Glasgow ~~2006 *Pattern Language: Clothing as Communicator* (group exh.), Art Museum at UC Santa Barbara ~~2005 *Lucy Orta* (solo exh.), Barbican, London ~~1999 *Lucy Orta: Grafisches Kabinett* (solo exh.), Secession, Vienna

Susan Taber Avila
b. 1960, Texas (America); lives in Oakland (America)
~~~~~ Selected Exhibitions: 2006 *Shoe Stories* (solo exh.), Contemporary Crafts Museum and Gallery, Portland ~~2003 *All Sewn Up* (solo exh.), The Sturm Gallery, Reno

Mark Newport
b. 1964, Amsterdam (The Netherlands); lives in Mesa (America)
~~~~~ Selected Exhibitions: 2006 *Mark Newport: Superheroics* (solo exh.), San Diego State University Art Gallery, San Diego ~~2005 *Hanging by a Thread* (group exh.), The Moore Space, Miami

Matthew Barney
b. 1967, San Francisco (America); lives in New York (America)
~~~~~ Selected Exhibitions: 2006 *Matthew Barney: Drawing Restraint* (solo exh.), San Francisco Museum of Modern Art, San Francisco ~~2003 *Matthew Barney: The Cremaster Cycle* (solo exh.), Solomon R Guggenheim Museum, New York

Mike Kelley
b. 1954, Detroit (America); lives in Los Angeles (America)
~~~~~ Selected Exhibitions: 2008 *Cut Felt Banners* (solo exh.), 1018 Art, New York ~~2008 *The Puppet Show* (group exh.), ICA Institute of Contemporary Art, Philadelphia ~~2006 *Mike Kelley: Profondeurs Vertes* (solo exh.), Louvre, Paris ~~2004 *Mike Kelley: The Uncanny* (group exh.), Tate Liverpool, Liverpool

Nick Cave
b. Missouri (America); lives in Chicago (America)
~~~~~ Selected Exhibitions: 2007 *Second Skins* (solo exh.), Jacksonville Museum of Contemporary Art, Florida ~~2006 *SOUNDSUITS* (solo exh.), Chicago Cultural Center, Chicago

Paddy Hartley
b. 1970, West Yorkshire (Britain); lives in London (Britain) / www.projectfacade.com
~~~~~ Selected Exhibitions: 2007 *Faces of Battle* Project Facade Exhibition (artist and co-curator), National Army Museum, London ~~2002 *Short Cuts To Beauty* (solo exh.), The Victoria and Albert Museum, London

Magdalena Abakanowicz
b. 1930, Falenty (Poland); lives in Warsaw (Poland)
~~~~~ Selected Exhibitions: 2006 *Magdalena Abakanowicz* (solo exh.), Marlborough Monaco, Monaco ~~2006 *Magdalena Abakanowicz* (solo exh.), Trondheim Art Museum, Trondheim ~~2005 *Magdalena Abakanowicz* (solo exh.), Museum of Fine Arts, Budapest

SPACES

Christo and Jeanne-Claude
Christo: b.1935, Gabrovo (Bulgaria); lives in New York (America) / Jeanne-Claude: b.1952, Casablanca (Morocco); lives in New York (America)
~~~~~ Select Installations: 2005 *The Gates*, Central Park, New York City ~~1999 *The Wall—13,000 Oil Barrels Gasometer*, Oberhausen, Germany 1999 ~~1997–1998 *Wrapped Trees*, Fondation Beyeler and Berower Park, Riehen, Switzerland

Craig Fisher
b. 1976, Joannesburg (Africa); lives in Nottingham and London (Britain)
~~~~~ Selected Exhibitions: 2007 *Textile 07—Kaunas Art Biennial* (group exh.), Kaunas ~~2007 *Hold your Fire* (solo exh.), Rokeby Gallery, London

Freddie Robins
b. 1965, Hitchin (Britain); lives in London (Britain)
~~~~~ Selected Exhibitions: 2005 *Ceremony*, Pump House Gallery, Battersea Park, London ~~2005 *Knit 2 Together: Concepts in Knitting*, Crafts Council Gallery, London and touring

Laura Vickerson
b. 1959, Edmonton (Canada); lives in Calgary (Canada)
~~~~~ Selected Exhibitions: 2002 *William's Carnations*, Site Specific Installation, Textile Museum, Toronto ~~2000 Biennale de Quebec (group exh.), Québec

Seamus McGuinness
b. 1964, Donegal (Ireland); lives in Ballyvaughan (Ireland)
~~~~~ Selected Exhibitions: 2007 *Textile 07 Kaunas Art Biennial,* Kaunas ~~2005 *21g* (solo exh.), various locations, Ireland

Mary Tuma
b. 1961 Oakland (Canada); lives in North Carolina (America)
~~~~~ Selected Exhibitions: 2007 *Homes for the Disembodied II* (solo exh.), Crocker Art Museum, Sacramento (Canada) ~~2007 *Textile Monuments* (group exh.), Green Hill Centre for NC Art, Greensboro

Susie MacMurray
b. 1959, London (Britain); lives in Manchester (Britain)
~~~~~ Selected Exhibitions: 2006 *Shell* (solo exh.), Pallant House Gallery, Chichester ~~2006 *Echo* (solo exh.), York St Mary's, York Museums Trust, York

Jennifer Angus
b. 1961, Edmonton (Canada); lives in Wisconsin (America)
~~~~~ Selected Exhibitions: 2007 *Shadow Ball* (group exh.), Art Gallery of Ontario, Toronto ~~2006 *A Terrible Beauty* (solo exh.), Textile Museum of Canada, Toronto

Yinka Shonibare
b. 1962, London (Britain); lives in London (Britain)
~~~~~ Selected Exhibitions: 2007 *Scratch the Surface* (solo exh.), National Gallery, London ~~2004 *Yinka Shonibare* (solo exh.), The Fabric Workshop and Museum, Philadelphia ~~2003 *Play with me 9* (solo exh.), Stephen Friedman Gallery, London

Acknowledgements

We would like to extend our sincerest gratitude to all of the artists who applied to be a part of this book, the wealth of exciting and inspiring material we received was completely amazing, and we could not have undertaken this project without the input and enthusiasm of everyone involved.
~~~~~ To Jann Haworth, whose work helped to introduce the art world to the idea of textiles as fine art, and who graciously agreed to use her voice to introduce this volume, our debt extends far beyond the scope of this book.
~~~~~ To Janis Jefferies and Bradley Quinn, whose words awakened this book to the conflicts and celebrations alive in textile art, and whose advice and direction were an invaluable resource throughout the process of the project.
~~~~~ To Nikos Kotsopoulos, without whom this volume wouldn't have been possible, and to Lucy Gundry, Aimee Selby, Raven Smith, Blanche Craig, Adam Thompson, Julius Pasteiner and Caraline Douglas for their insightful texts, and to Camille Chauchat for her technical help with the images. Finally, to Rachel Pfleger for giving this fascinating material shape with her sensitive and beautiful design.

© 2008 BLACK DOG PUBLISHING LIMITED, LONDON, UK, the artists and authors. All rights reserved

Texts by Janis Jefferies, Bradley Quinn, Nikos Kotsopoulos, Nadine Monem, Lucy Gundry, Aimee Selby, Raven Smith, Blanche Craig, Adam Thompson, Julius Pasteiner and Caraline Douglas

Editor: Nadine Käthe Monem
Assistant Editor: Nikolaos Kotsopoulos
Designer: Rachel Pfleger

Black Dog Publishing Limited
10A Acton Street
WC1X 9NG
London UK

T.   +44 (0)20 713 5097
F.   +44 (0)20 713 8682
E.   info@blackdogonline.com

All opinions expressed within this publication are those of the author and not necessarily of the publisher.

British Library Cataloguing-in-Publication Data.
A CIP record for this book is available from the British Library.

ISBN   978 1 906155 29 2

BLACK DOG PUBLISHING LIMITED, LONDON, UK, is an environmentally responsible company. *Contemporary Textiles: The Fabric of Fine Art* is printed on Sappi Magno Satin, a chlorine-free certified paper.

architecture art design
fashion history photography
theory and things

black dog
publishing

london uk

www.blackdogonline.com